By Heart/De Memoria

*Cuban Women's Journeys
In and Out of Exile*

By Heart/ De Memoria

Cuban Women's Journeys In and Out of Exile

Edited by
María de los Angeles Torres

 Temple University Press
Philadelphia

Temple University Press, Philadelphia 19122
Copyright © 2003 by Temple University
All rights reserved
Published 2003
Printed in the United States of America

Library of Congress Cataloging-in-Publication Data

By heart/de memoria ; Cuban women's journeys in and out of exile / edited by
María de los Angeles Torres.
    p. cm.
  Includes bibliographical references.
  ISBN 1-59213-010-0 (cloth : alk. paper)—ISBN 1-59213-011-9 (pbk. : alk. paper)
    1. Cuban American women—Biography. 2. Exiles—Cuba—Biography.
I. Title: Cuban woman's journeys in and out of exile. II. Torres, María de los
Angeles.

  E184.C97 B94 2003
  972.9106'4'0922—dc21

2002073202

This book is dedicated to María Isabel Vigil (my mother) and to all our mothers, who nurtured our hearts, and to the memory of Lourdes Casal, Ana Mendieta, and Raquel Mendieta Costa, who, despite their deaths, continue to form part of our bridges.

Contents

Preface

IN THE spring of 1993 I was on my way to Cuba with Nereida García-Ferraz, a friend with whom I had made the journey many times. Changes in both Cuban and U.S. policies sometimes facilitated a return to the island, and at other times made it impossible. It was the latter case that spring. We had been promised a reentry permit to the island by a Cuban functionary who had since lost her job in a political purge. Nonetheless, we headed to Miami, hoping that the permit would arrive anyway. (This was not the first time that we waited in Miami until the very last day to learn whether our trip would be allowed.) Once in Miami, it became clear that we would not be able to travel to the island. We suddenly had two unplanned weeks in the city we considered enemy territory, for it was here in Miami that our lives were threatened when we had returned to the island earlier.

Miami had just been a point of transfer for us, a place in which we feared spending time because of terrorist acts against those who traveled to Cuba, but now the city was changing. We found many of our friends from the island living there. The coming of our contemporaries from Cuba to Miami necessarily forced us to reconceptualize both the nation and exile. Meanwhile, we were witnessing the coming of age of the second generation of Cuban exiles already living in Miami, who had a sense of entitlement about making their voices heard there. We found ourselves in the curious position of knowing both the world of recent arrivals and the world of those who were raised in the United States. Although we had been in some ways outsiders to both worlds, we were part of both. Miami became the place where we could actually talk and rethink our relationship to the island, the exile community, and ourselves.

What we found initially was common ground, converging visions that crossed the Straits of Florida in both directions. Certain events marked our journey; there were common points of reference, particularly moments of illusion and disillusion. There were differences as well, a broken conga line, discontinuity. A project of national reconciliation needed to be based on an understanding of our differences, not just our commonalties. Throughout these various times, the women seemed able to talk more openly than the men about the ambiguities and the changes that were occurring in our lives. We did not feel a need to defend old political positions, nor deny them, for that matter. Rather, we needed to explore the ambiguous zones, to disagree, to look at our histories and ourselves in ways that helped us to understand how we could continue to engage with the people and places we loved so deeply without losing ourselves in the process. We did not pretend to make statements for anyone; we were just trying to find our moorings.

It had been women from many different perspectives, after all, who had played important roles in forging a paradigm of politics and identity that was inclusive of both home and host countries, mindful of multiple points of reference. Surely, men have been involved,[1] but women have been most critical to the endeavor and have seldom been recognized publicly. Lourdes Casal, a poet and sociologist who reconciled her exile by returning to and dying in Cuba, made the most dangerous and difficult journey, the first return to the island. She built a bridge that has allowed all of us to return.

María Cristina Herrera, founder and director of the Instituto de Estudios Cubanos, was instrumental in promoting a dialog with the Cuban government. Marifeli Pérez-Stable, a founder of the Antonio Maceo Brigade and *Areíto,* forged a vision of unity. Mariana Gastón, Miren Uriarte, Ana María García, Vivian Otero, Dagmaris Cabezas, and Rosario Moreno sought links through the Antonio Maceo Brigade. Alicia Torres for years headed a committee that lobbied for normal diplomatic relations between the United States and Cuba. In Spain, Anabel Rodríguez had done the same. Hilda Diez helped run a travel agency that chartered flights to the island, Silvia Wilhelm continues to work with Puentes a Cuba, and Elly Vilano Chovel opened the past for Operation Pedro Pan children and extended a hand, through the Catholic Church, to those who were still on the island.

Within the academic and cultural worlds, Ruth Behar, Eliana Rivera, Sonia Rivera, Iraida López, and Cristina Nosti all worked on various projects aimed at building bridges, oftentimes at great personal sacrifice, as has been the case of María Romeu, who promoted island music before the Buena Vista Social Club phenomenon and was red-baited from her job at MTV Latino. Then there were the visual artists, such as Ana Mendieta, whose earth sculptures, slowly weathering into the caves of Jaruco and Varadero, testified to her return, and Mercedes Wanguemert, whose paintings and installations explore her obsession, as well as ours, with the island. Playwrights such as María Irene Fornés and Dolores Prida wrote about the intimate sides of exile, nation, and identity. Carmelita Tropicana returns to the island to recapture her lost memory in her play, "Milk of Amnesia," Most recently, Carmen Peláez, a young Cuban born in Miami who defines herself as an exile, has provided intimate glimpses into women's experiences with the revolution and its aftermath in her one-woman performance, "Rum and Coke." Women writers such as Achy Obejas and Cristina García have returned as well. In *Dreaming in Cuban,* García's main character, Pilar, returns to the island, and Celia, her grandmother, who has stayed behind, gives her the task of remembering for the nation. Pilar is an active exile, engaged with the island, not one drowning in nostalgia. In Obejas' novel *Days of Awe,* the very essence of Cuban culture is reexamined through the lens of the Jewish diaspora, thus widening and deepening the sense of cultural heterogeneity on the island and in the exile community.

This anthology has come to life with the support of many. Most importantly, the students in my class on Diasporas: The Politics of Gender and Identity, have renewed my enthusiasm to combine teaching and research with compassion and theoretical exigencies. Claudia Gomez, Stephanie Hoehne, and Ashley Gegg helped with research and preparation of the manuscript.

Doris Braendel had faith in the project, and the staff at Temple University Press followed through. Charlotte Sheedy and Neeti Madan encouraged and supported its publication. Patricia Boero and Woody Wickham, formerly of the John D. and Catherine T. MacArthur Foundation, made the initial grant to support the project. Bill Díaz, formerly at the Ford Foundation, facilitated the actual grant made by Rebecca Nichols. Lisandro Pérez and Uva de Aragón hosted our first public encounter at the Cuban Research Institutes' conference in Miami. Quizqueya Enríquez and Consueló Castañeda provided many insights. Achy Obejas read and made important editorial comments on the manuscript. Lisa Milam-Pérez and Eliana Rivera made invaluable comments as well. Translation from Spanish to English was done by David Frey and from English to Spanish by Eduardo Aparicio. Without their talent to build a linguistic bridge, this anthology could not exist. Raquelin Mendieta gave permission to use her sister's artwork on the cover of the paperback edition and supported the project in a very important way.

To Matt Piers, my husband, and Alejandra and Paola Piers-Torres, thank you for your love.

To the authors who have so generously and unselfishly shared their memories and opened their / our hearts, I give my thanks for their trust. Someone asked how the writers to this volume were chosen. At first there was a conscious effort to have representative writers from the island and from the exile community, but these lines were constantly blurring as writers whom I had asked to contribute started leaving the island. There was also an attempt to present a chronology of the exile community by having people who left at different times. Most importantly, though, were the personal connections that we had with each other through which we were able to defy the restrictions that both governments placed on our getting to know each other.

I place this book in the tradition forged by women seeking political and personal reconciliation, the same tradition forged by so many women on the island and in exile, including our mothers, who refused to sever ties with their relatives or their histories. We know that this book cannot yet be published in Cuba. It's not that women on the island do not strive to shorten the distance between us, but exile is still a forbidden place, and to recognize it or engage with it outside the official channels has been simply impermissible.[2] It is our deepest desire to be able to return to the island to bring together the authors of these essays, to engage them in the same way we have been able to gather in Miami to discuss gender, identities, and politics of diaspora and nation and to share our personal stories with each other.

Notes

1. Among the publications written by men seeking to understand the Other are Román de la Campa (*Cuba on My Mind: Journeys to a Severed Nation*. New York: Verso Press, 2000), who writes about his journey; Juan Pablo Balaster, María Elena Escalona, and Iván de la Nuez (*La Isla posible*. Barcelona: Ediciones Destino, 1995). Also see *Encuentro,* edited by Jesús Díaz in Madrid, Spain. There have also been a series of aesthetic projects, such as Eduardo Aparicio's photo exhibit, *Entre Miami y La Habana.*

2. On the island Pablo Armando Fernández has always provided a bridge (*Los niños se despiden*. La Habana: Editorial Casa de las Américas, 1968). Most recently the walls in Cuba have started to come down a bit. *Vigía,* published in Matanzas, was the first publication to publish authors who had left. Ambrosio Fornet has advocated for including voices from exile in publications (*Memorias recobradas*. Santa Clara, Cuba: Ediciones Capro, 2000). Víctor Fowler (*Rupturas y homenajes*. La Habana: UNEAC, 1998), has explored the other side, as has Jorge Luis Arcos (*De los inferos*. La Habana: UNEAC, 1999). Most explicit has been the work of visual artists such as Los Carpinteros, Kcho, and especially Tania Bruguera, whose work is included in this anthology.

1

Introduction

María de los Angeles Torres

"BY HEART," in English, *"de memoria,"* in Spanish: Both suggest memories that can be recalled with ease, as well as those that contain intimate knowledge of past events or people. These essays are written from that intimate place of memory, not from the ease of recollection. The authors were born in Cuba, an island/nation only ninety miles from the United States. Our lives were forever altered by a revolution in 1959 that captured the political imagination of all those who dreamed of a future marked by social justice.

We had been an island nation bounded by a seawall floating between seemingly contradictory coasts, sometimes Europe and the New World, other times North and South America. However, the revolution unfolded in the era of the Cold War, whose geographical concerns insisted on placing an island in the Caribbean at the center of a struggle between East and West, communism and capitalism. This great, global ideological fault line has made it difficult to explore the divisions within our nation, which in our experiences ran much deeper. In this new conflict, our moorings were unhitched, and el *malecón,* the Havana seawall that hugs the central part of the city and is such an intimate part of our national iconography, went from containing a nation to dividing its people. Staying or leaving became a litmus test to prove loyalty and ultimately *cubanía*. For those in exile, the island was forbidden, just as the exile was off limits to those on the island. The Other was erased from official memory, as travel was prohibited by both states, communications were made almost impossible, and exchanges were criminalized. For the island and the exile, collective and personal memories became a militarized zone sharply demarcated and jealously guarded by those bidding for power.

This book brings together the voices and images of women who have met during their unauthorized travels beyond these boundaries. Some of the authors have lived most of their lives on the island, others in exile; some have only recently left the island. Each post-revolution exile generation is represented: the Operation Pedro Pan generation of the 1960s, the Freedom Flights of the 1970s, the Mariel boat lift of the 1980s, and the "low intensity" exiles of the 1990s, thus providing a personal chronology of exile history.[1] Some of the authors have been able to return to the island for long periods; others have been refused reentry by the Cuban government. Those writing from the island witnessed each exodus and each return. They too have spent time abroad exploring the forbidden exile. We have all endured separations from parents, children, family, and friends.

Our encounters with our Others gave us an opportunity to meet and build relations with our counterparts on the island/in exile. We have found among us common ground as well as differences, and we have developed shared points of references. In the process, we learned that we could not make sense of either our past or our present with only militarized conceptions of our identities. We felt constrained by rigid identity schemes, particularly those tied to notions of singular nation-states or implacable political programs. These essays chronicle our travels outside the geographical and ideological confines of nation and exile, boundaries demarcated by two feuding states in the Cold War era. They are also searches for more complex frameworks with which to make sense of identity(ies) that were not exclusively rooted in either host or home countries; in one of two political dogmas, in solely the intellect or the heart.

Perhaps our revolution and its exiles are unique. They are embedded in a long history of external and internal exiles. The Cuban nation, its landscapes, physicality, and spiritual values were imagined from the distant gaze of exile *(la lejanía),* causing certain anxiety about its precise location. The nation is imagined from abroad in the poetry of José María Heredia and Gertrudis Gómez de Avellaneda.[2] Félix Varela and José Martí envisioned the modernist nation from the United States. An U.S. invasion interrupted this utopian dream, and thus, the United States acquired a unique place in the island's history, and Cuba and its exiles would come to occupy a central location in the colonial imagination of the Right and the Left. Perhaps it is this relationship, coupled with the dramatic moment in world history in which the Cuban revolution occurred, and the moment of rupture in U.S. society unfolding at the time of our emigration, that make us think of our national destiny and our displacement as exceptional. But our search for nationhood and the consequent displacement of people are not unique. After all, the twentieth century in part is defined by political struggles for independent nation-states that then engendered authoritarian regimes. Nationalism has an essential association with exile.[3] Exile, after all, is the antithesis of nation. It creates a strongly knit community based on commonality, whereas exile represents those who are different. Exiles, in turn, also erect tightly woven places with clearly demarcated boundaries.

Cuban nationalism also shares similar gendering processes with other movements, which in turn placed women in a potentially oppositional location. The struggle for independence of modern nation-states was often symbolized through feminine imagery[4]—a woman draped in the national flag unshackling the chains of colonialism. However, these movements gave rise to a modern form of patriarchy in which the state (note that in Spanish it is preceded by a masculine adjective: *el estado)* assumed authority over the nation (family): *la nacion* and *la familia,* both preceded by a feminine adjective.

In its most severe form, these patriarchal states became authoritarian and demanded nothing less than complete loyalty as a condition for membership. The disloyal were banished and the loyal prohibited from having contact with those who had left. In the case of Cuba, travel within the island as well as to and from the island was restricted and monitored. Cuba became one of the few countries in the world in which its citizens had to ask for permission to return to visit as well as to travel abroad. Although travel in modernity can be construed in many ways,[5] in this case it became a means to defy the official order. Women, in particular, were the ones to travel to maintain contact with their relatives.

Each journey, in its own way, challenged the foundations of the boundaries, which defined who we are. The essays do not attempt to present a new cartography, but perhaps one more nuanced. Internal and external exiles provoke a particular gaze,[6] perhaps a more complex understanding of our realities, which provide new ways of thinking even about nations.[7] Our purpose here, however, is to suggest different ways, not new ways, of defining nations, more layered, definitely more intimate ways of defining/ becoming who we may be.

Contesting the Boundaries of Exiles and Nations

Our travels are aquatic, fluid, and thus the volume opens with "The Boat" (*"El Bote"*), a poem written by Achy Obejas, whose family made the journey from Cuba to the United States in a small boat. She writes, "we don't seem to leave the country, you and I, always with an open map, searching the borders and open coasts."

What is the difference between exile and nation? Liz Balmaseda begins her poetic appreciation of Miami by stating, " It is, at its most luminous stretch, a reflection." "Havana, twinkles in Miami." While growing up in the main port of entry for Cuban exiles, the island existed for Liz "only in the most poetic terms." Thus begins the search for a space between memory and reflection where the clearly demarcated political boundaries between exile and nation blur.

If exile is to live in a place where there is no house in which we were children,[8] nation must be the place where this house still exists. Why does *home* have to be constructed in one geographical place? Indeed, the homes of our childhood stand erect in our memories and remain intact when we revisit them as adults. Even their sizes as we remember them from childhood remain intact in our memories, although they are in reality much smaller when we re-experience them as adults. Thus nations also live in our memories, not only in politically fractured geographical zones.

I was sent to the United States unaccompanied, at the age of six, through a secret U.S. State Department–coordinated operation named Pedro Pan. In my essay "Where Ghosts Dance *el Guaguancó*," I write about how my search for home first led me back to the island with the Antonio Maceo Brigade. "The homecomings were intense. We had a sense of mission and community, which bonded our generation in a very special way. . . .We were a political phenomenon, children of the exile returning home." Over the next few years, I was to experience a deep sense of disillusionment, which paradoxically I shared with my newfound friends on the island. I came to understand that the political culture that drove me away from the exile community also characterized those in power on the island. Still, I did not want to renounce the island, my nation, nor did I want to accept exile on its terms; rather, I needed a place in which I could bring together these seemingly contradictory parts of who I am and who I wanted to be. I found this place outside the state institutions, a place where nations are fluid, where they are sustained by collective and personal recollections. Nations are, after all, our souls. They are where our past and present meet to imagine a future, create new homes.

We typically think of the boundaries of nations almost exclusively in terms of geography.[9] Exiles are bound by that geography as well, because it becomes a point of reference. Maybe it is easier for those bidding for power to lay claim to a physical territory than to control the other components that constitute nationhood.

Geography is also experienced personally, however. Nereida García-Ferraz' family made the decision to leave the island in the early 1960s but were not able to depart until 1970. She remembers the time that preceded her "Freedom Flight": "I learned to keep my eyes fixed on the landscape: I knew that one fine day I wouldn't be there anymore, so I enjoyed it all in a very special way, as if to keep it from escaping my memory." It was the images of her relatives in the 1950s that "helped me rebuild myself, to place pieces of the puzzle, searching always for that bigger image that will help me understand what paths everyone took to get to the places they are today." The photographs of her relatives helped inform her sense of family geography, for "they bring the consolation of knowing that, at one time, my family had lived whole eras in a single place, had belonged to a place: the island." By returning, Nereida was able to reconnect with both her family and her landscape.

For many of us displaced from our homeland our greatest desire was to return there to live, but the Cuban government would only permit us to visit. Yet our visits, taking place after nearly twenty years of exile from Cuba, had a tremendous impact on the island nonetheless. *55 Hermanos,* a documentary film about the first group of young exiles permitted to visit the island, caused a sensation in Cuba. The book account, *Contra viento y marea,* won the testimonial literary prize from Casa de las Américas. Both in the exile community and on the island, those of us who traveled back to Cuba represented the antithesis of the official positions. Our travels dispelled the myth of irreconcilable, separate realities. For the exile community, our returns somehow questioned the essence of exile—that is that you cannot return. We were met by an extreme terrorist backlash. For the island, we were living proof that Cubans lived outside the boundaries of the state, thus challenging the state's authority to de-nationalize those who left. The Cuban government kept close tabs on us.

Our travels provided us with an opportunity to establish a human link with our homeland. Two great poets, Eliseo Diego and Pablo Armando Fernández, opened their homes to *los Brigadistas.* Their daughters, Teresa de Jesús Fernández and Josefina de Diego, became my close friends. For Teresa de Jesús Fernández, the boundaries between nation and exile were edged in her sense of self, not in geography or ideology. Her passage from childhood into adolescence and the loss of innocence were intricately interwoven with the departure of her best friends into exile. In "From This Side of the Fish Tank" (the glassed-in passenger waiting area at the airport), she remembers, "Some of my most wrenching memories belongs to this stage in my life: the last night we slept under the same roof. This was the beginning of an endless incision." "Exile," she explains, "tends to be seen as *des-tierro* (landless); seen this way, it is only those who leave who suffer." For her, this is an incomplete definition, for it does not include "the Other; the internal exile who is left with the estrangement." If the departure of her friends edged a painful incision, the return of young exiles marked her passage into adulthood. Teresa was at first ambivalent about the returning youth; after all, we were allowed to criticize the government in a manner that would incur punishment for those on the island. She "discovered that they had a different way of looking at things; more than just seeing them, they imprinted them." At first she did not understand this process, but when she thought that someday she might be in their place, "I started being more careful about the way I experienced my own city." She now lives and works in Italy most of the year.

Josefina "Fefé" de Diego's family had almost left the island in the early 1960s, which marked them forever with the "original sin" of having once thought about leaving. Her curiosity about what could have been her parallel life in the United States drew her to the returning young exiles. In her essay "Through Other Looking Glasses" she reflects on how her family history contributed to her more fluid view of her Other as well as her sense of time itself. Fefé knew well the dynamics of displaced geographical memories. Her grandmother had spent ten years in New York as a child. She had taught English to her son, Eliseo, "because she couldn't imagine his company without finding that odd underground river of communication that can only be established through the nuances of one's first language." For Fefé, languages both bound and blurred her nation and its boundaries and changed her sense of time. "For me," she writes, "meeting some of these young people has meant recovering very dear friends, friends who, as my father would say, enlarge time for us."

For the Cuban public in general, the government's reversal of its long-standing policy of keeping exiles off the island was traumatic as well. Unlike the U.S. press, which had heralded the successes of the "golden exile," the Cuban media was mostly silent on the exile community, except for periodic reports of how poor life was for them in the United States. This image was shattered after more than 125,000 exiles returned to the island in 1979 to visit relatives. Regardless of how difficult life was in the United States, the exile community as a whole had more access to consumer goods than did residents of the island. Political and economic discontent began to rise.

In April of 1980, shortly after the Cuban government announced that those wanting to leave could do so through the Peruvian Embassy, thousands of people jammed the compound beyond capacity. Finally, an arrangement was made to transport refugees to the United States through the Cuban port of Mariel. Mariel cut to the core. The island again split wide open as those who stayed were encouraged by the government to organize *Actos de repudio* (Acts of Repudiation) in the homes of those who were leaving. The official boundaries between nation and exile were once again reinforced. Those who left via Mariel became known as *Marielitos*. Ironically, both the Cuban state—and the U.S. media—constructed images coincided to portray *Marielitos* as *la escoria* (the undesirable scum).

Beyond this ideologically driven image were the individuals who became the new exiles. In "La Salida: The Departure," Mirta Ojito describes how the departure plan unfolded for her family. In retelling her story she asks, What is the essence of one's identity? Mirta was sixteen at the time that her parents decided to leave via Mariel. Her account of the fourteen days before her departure document the process of shedding all those familiar points of reference that define who we are and where home resides. Mirta writes, "A home is a hard place to abandon. Where does one end and the home begin? Are treasured possessions just things?" After her family left behind their material belongings they were taken by police car to a makeshift detention center called El Mosquito, which Mirta describes as "the final stop to strip us of our identity and possessions." It was here that people were clustered by different categories and classified according to which boats would take them to the United States. "From then on, our names become unimportant. The Valley Chief had become our new identity."

Carmen Díaz recounts her own Mariel departure in her essay, "The Recurring Dream." As a young girl she believed in the utopian dream of the revolution and thought, "I would have loved, secretly and with such passion, to have joined the guerrillas. I would be a guerrillera." In 1978, Carmen was teaching physics at the University of Havana. Revolutions, after all, should be a continual process of reflection and criticism, and it was in the hard sciences that critical thinking flourished at the time. Soon she realized that the regime would not permit this. Carmen writes, "I left because that world became too narrow for me." But *Marielitos* were met with contempt in the United States. The same authoritarian political culture they had hoped to leave behind was also institutionalized in the exile community, and two feuding states that "play the immigration question like a game of ping pong without paying much attention to how they were tearing people apart were costing me my life." Carmen had left two young daughters behind, thinking that it would only be a matter of months before she could reclaim them. Carmen writes, "Time is irretrievable." She dreamed repeatedly of saying goodbye to her two young daughters and to her hopes of being part of a revolutionary dream.

Young exiles returning home physically crossed paths with a generation that was leaving. We still believed in the utopian vision, whereas they were beginning to view exile as a viable alternative to what had become their lost dream. Yet the more time we spent in Cuba, the more aware we became of how corrupt the system was. We also met a generation on the island, intellectuals, and artists of the 1980s, and as trust began to build, we shared our disillusionment with these friends. The 1989 Arnaldo Ochoa Sánchez trial and his execution became a defining moment. The increasingly transparent ideological veil that had given a sense of coherence to the revolution project unraveled. We scrambled to make sense of the moment as well as the past. For those on the island, part of this process meant recouping what had been lost, including what was lost in exile. Initially, many tried to do this by engaging in an intellectual and aesthetic contestation of power on the island as we were trying to do through exchange programs, but we soon discovered the limits to this endeavor. Exile soon became a condition that defined not only those outside of the national territory, but also those inside as well. The Ochoa trial left no doubt that claims of democracy and justice were official deceptions. Dreams and illusions dissolved into stark and hopeless reality. Islanders, just as exiles, realized their impotence, for few had access or permission to construct the collective project that now imposed a collective memory and future and a grim one at that.

In "Only Fragments of Memory," Raquel Mendieta Costa recalls "that if anything defines the way I looked at the world during the first years of the Revolution, it is amazement." For a young girl, the early 1960s were years of wonderment. Although some of her relatives left for the North, her family stayed. In her essay she weaves fragments of her memories about political and personal events. Throughout, she explores the contradictions in the promises of the revolutionary government and her personal experiences living with the consequences of decision made by those who held the reigns of power. In contrast to the heroic tales of success, which she parallels with her own experiences as a competitive swimmer, she offers a personal account of the failure of the collective project. In offering her version, she in effect questions how history itself is constructed. Raquel's break with official history took her to exile as ours had taken us back to the island.

In "Words Without Borders," Madelín Cámara explores her journey in search of a Third Option, neither exile nor the island's political model. Madelín, a member of what has been called *La Generación de los Ochenta*, the 1980s Generation, left the island in search of philosophical positions not rooted in either side of the geographical/philosophical divide of Miami/Havana in which she could explore a new paradigm.[10] She begins her essay by stating, "The history of an exile does not begin the day we leave the country, but on the day we feel that the country has abandoned us." Her first departure was to Mexico, a neutral zone that at the time was home to over 4,000 Cuban intellectuals, artists, and writers, but pressure from the Cuban government soon forced her to cross into the United States.

Tania Bruguera, a visual artist, was one of the first on the island to explore the loss felt on the island when people left. Exile as a forced physical separation severs contact with the familiar points of reference that contribute to the creation and sustenance of memory. It also alters the landscape for those who stay behind. To explore the loss of exile was somehow to violate the official stand that the revolution was stronger and purer, without those who left. Very few academics were even permitted to write about the community abroad. The impact of the exodus of the 1990s was dramatic. Thousands of people left on makeshift rafts, and hundreds of intellectuals, artists, musicians, writers, and filmmakers made their way to "third countries." Tania began her journey to understand exile through the work of Ana Mendieta, an artist who had emigrated to the United States as part of Operation Pedro Pan. She, too, had returned to Cuba to work. After her death, little was said about her work on the island. Tania recreated Ana's work to recover for the nation its parts, which lived in exile. She continued exploring the sense of loss through a multifaceted project, Memory of the Postwar Period *(Memorias de la posguerra)*, which began as an unofficial publication that dealt openly and honestly with the loss that exile leaves on the island and the longing for those who leave nostalgia in reverse, some could say. Yet this project was short-lived; the official world censored it.

Ana's work is on the cover of our paperback edition. A cloth washed ashore finds an anchor on a piece of driftwood. Our journeys have made us who we are.

This book, which began in Miami looking toward the island, ends on the island as it gazes toward the exile community through her work. These are our journeys to nations and exiles, forbidden places for each of us yet deeply etched in our beings. Exiles and nations, after all, are constructions intimately woven into memories, recollections, and dreams. As all human constructions, they can be bound and unbound and even reconfigured through an ongoing process of reflection, confrontation, and creation.

Notes

1. The post-revolutionary Cuban exodus was commonly classified by different waves defined by mode of entry and exit. These have included early exiles (1959–1961), when entry into the United States was facilitated by an extensive visa waiver program that ended at the time of the October Missile Crisis; the Freedom Flights (1965–1973), begun as a response to the Cuban government's opening of the port of Camarioca and permitting anyone wanting to pick up relatives to do so; Mariel (1980–1984), another opening of a port in Cuba and consequently, another immigration treaty; the Balsero crisis and low-intensity exile (1987–1995); and the present.

2. Vitier, Cintio. 1970. *Lo cubano en la poesía*. La Habana: Instituto del Libro.

3. Said, Edward. 2000. *Reflections on Exile and Other Essay*, pp. 176–77. Cambridge, Mass.: Harvard University Press.

4. Kaplan, Caren, Norma Alarcón, and Minoo Moallem, eds., 1999. *Between Woman and Nation: Nationalisms, Transnational Feminisms, and the State*. Durham: Duke University Press.

5. Kaplan, Caren. 1999. *Questions of Travel: Postmodern Discourses of Displacement*. Durham: Duke University Press.

6. Said, Edward. 1994. *Representations of the Intellectual*. New York: Vintage Books.

7. Kristeva, Julia. 1993. *Nations Without Nationalism*. New York: Columbia University Press.

8. Casal, Lourdes. 1981. *Definición*. In *Palabras juntan revolución*. La Habana: Casa de las Américas; English translation by David Frye, *Bridges to Cuba/Puentes a Cuba* (Ann Arbor: University of Michigan Press, 1995).

9. Phillips, Richard. 1977. *Mapping Men and Empires: A Geography of Adventure*. London: Routledge.

10. Homi Bhabhi, An Interview: Third Space. In Rutherford, Johnathan. 1991. *Identity, Community, Culture and Difference*, pp. 207–221. London: Lawrence & Wifhart.

2

The Boat

Achy Obejas

El Bote

no nos acabamos de ir del país
tú y yo, siempre con el mapa abierto
examinando las fronteras, costas abiertas
añorando playas perdidas
las olas tibias de amores anteriores
y la perfección de otros pasados
volvemos siempre al mismo punto
señalando flechas en diferentes direcciones
con todo propósito (el alivio, la razón
por la distancia y cercanía)
estamos siempre al punto de partir
pretendiendo frío, indiferencia
practicando pequeños argumentos
con el futuro
y falta de memoria con nuestro pasado
pero la prueba está en el mapa
gastado como una sábana que ha visto
muchas noches

The Boat

we don't seem to leave the country
you and I, always with an open map
searching the borders and open coasts
yearning for lost shores
the warm waters of former loves
and the perfection of yesterday
we always come back to the same point
aiming arrows in different directions
deliberately (the relief, the reason
for the distance and proximity)
we're always at a point of departure
pretending coolness, indifference
practicing trivial arguments
with the future
and a lack of memory
but the proof is in the map
worn like a bed sheet
after too many nights

3

Reflections

Liz Balmaseda

IT IS, AT its most luminous stretch, a reflection. In its lights and arches, in its shrines and labyrinths, in its exuberance and anguish, it is a reflection. Havana twinkles in Miami, its music echoes along the streets of exile, its spirit moves throughout the parlors of the elite, the kitchens of the working class.

It is always there: Cuba. Nothing has been sufficiently powerful to erase its presence or to co-opt the culture. Like the salty air from the sea that connects the island and the diaspora, it is there. In four decades of exodus and exile, this transported spirit of Cuba has risen in a complex city, my city. When I was growing up in Hialeah, the sprawling industrial city just north of Miami that later came to be known as *La ciudad que progresa,* I could see Cuba all over the place. I could find Cuba even on Thanksgiving Day, the most American of holidays, in the *frijoles negros* that steamed next to the perfect foreign cylinder of cranberry jelly. But it existed only in the most poetic terms. It was a place where the palm tree trunks were whiter, more beautiful even than the soaring royal palm trees that stood guard at the Hialeah racetrack. It was a place where the beaches were lovelier, better than any beach along any old Miami strip. The sugar was sweeter, the air cleaner, the seashells more stunning. Cuba was so breathtaking, and its absence so devastating, that everyone would cry when the Cuban

National Anthem was played at the *Añorada Cuba Show* each year. Even I, who had landed in Miami as an infant, who could not remember the palm trees or the sugar, who could not describe the seaside band shell in my native Puerto Padre, who did not even know the words to the Cuban National Anthem, cried, too. Cuba was that big.

I grew up believing Cuba was a place that existed only in black and white and exact shades of gray. It was as if all of my relatives on the island existed in another dimension, a kind of grainy freeze-frame. It was one giant prison, Cuba. Its black and white brutality—what kind of place would forbid my mother's parents from coming to Miami?—contrasted sharply with the colors and sounds of my world. My world was full of rumba and reds, passionate debates about communism, and frequent exhortations to fight for *libertad*. And all this thunder for Cuba resounded against a larger landscape of American pop culture.

I came to believe no other immigrant population in this country has been more scrutinized, analyzed, and less homogenized than Cuban Miami. Perhaps that is because ours is not an immigrant community. It has been called a true enclave. It is often said, with some exaggeration, that one can live and die in Cuban Miami without speaking a word of English. Perhaps that is an oversimplification, but it serves to illustrate a rare independence and a certain detachment from other Latino communities.

Our particular identity has been that we are exiles. At the risk of isolation from the streams of assimilation, we are *el exilio,* a banner that has brought on charges of arrogance and the wrath of the white flight stragglers. Not immigrants or émigrés or refugees, not documented or undocumented, we are exiles in a city built on nostalgia.

In our decades-old scramble not to forget, we have raised shrines, named streets, erected monuments, attempted replicas from memory and sepia prints. And stroke by stroke a landscape has taken shape, defined by streets named Ronald Reagan and Celia Cruz and *Añorada Cuba* (Cuba of My Yearning) Way, a park

Illustration 3.1. Liz Balmaseda, Miami, 1962

where old Cuban men play dominoes, a bayside shrine where recent refugees come to leave scraps of their rafts in gratitude at the feet of a *café-con-leche*–colored Virgin, a supermarket named Varadero. It is also defined by political riptides, an artistic and cultural renaissance, the identity struggles of the second generation, a language native to exile, pride, nostalgia, pain. It is deceivingly familiar, this place of royal palms and tropical fruit stands and Cuban flamingos and Cuban tile. It is not Cuba.

Just like Havana, Miami is Castrocentric. More than Republican or Democrat, black or white, male or female, Cuban Miami has revolved around the doings and undoings of Fidel Castro. For three and one-half decades he has been the axis upon which all good and evil, rage and reason, fact and fiction spin.

Just as it has kept the torch lit for the fatherland, the Castro obsession is also what has spawned Cuban Miami's darker side, the incidents of terrorism, the bouts of intolerance, the strong-arm power-brokering in the name of anti-Communism, the banning of musicians and writers and artists who are somehow identified with the Castro regime.

In consequence, an image of exile Miami as a knee-jerk, reactionary monolith has been hard to shake, even though the reality is different, a pluralistic, diverse community that is too often marred by a narrow extremist streak: There are working class parents who raise sons and daughters to be architects, developers, doctors, and lawyers; former Havana socialites who have been forced by the equalizing nature of exile to commingle in their elderly years with poor sugar mill workers and farmers; *batistianos* and the *fidelistas;* ex–political prisoners and celebrities; people who watched decades of their lives evaporate inside repressive, dank, Cuban prisons and their American children, grandchildren, and great-grandchildren. Luminaries of Castro's bohemian brat pack paint and write and ruminate in Miami. Yesterday's revolutionaries are today's checkout clerks. There are the young, identity-obsessed and often consumed by recapturing the long ago and far away, while nostalgia-bound older generations yearn for what once was.

I grew up thinking I was Cuban. It was why my mom wouldn't let me stay for sleepovers with the other Girl Scouts in my troop. It was why I was the only one in my troop who put sugar in hot chocolate. It must be because I'm Cuban, I used to think growing up in Hialeah. Cubans put sugar in everything. We even used to put it on top of buttered crackers. None of my American friends did that. They never sliced bananas into their red bean puree—well, they didn't even have red bean puree.

I was Cuban because I was different from the *americanito* kids in elementary school. They never seemed to have parties at their houses or any cousins. I had a ton of cousins because I was Cuban. Ours was a wounded population, and the wounds often have imposed an invisible structure, guiding political agendas, barring forgiveness, fanning intransigence.

Sometimes, life in Cuban Miami has too often seemed to be what we have while we don't have Cuba. At times if can be described as simply as absence of revolution. Yet, in this exile waiting room pulses a whole new history, a new culture amid the trappings of American life: government contracts, Miami Dolphin football games, real estate deals, marriages, graduations, happy hour, a deceiving air of assimilation.

Underneath it all, there is Cuba. It turns up as a bizarre foreign policy allusion in city commissioner races, as patriotic decor in car dealerships, in commercial jingles. We've created a new kind of hybrid culture between the magnified Havana of our memories and our dreams and the changed Miami of our reality. This is not merely a story of waiting. The impact of the exile presence has been enormous, politically, economically, culturally.

There are Cubans in Congress, in the state legislature, in the president's and vice-president's offices at colleges and universities, in the CEO's inner sanctum. We know the list: Gloria Estefan, Andy García, the late president of Coca Cola, Oscar Hijuelos. We have won Grammies, Emmies, genius grants. Our deeds have triggered important debates, not only about political action or U.S. foreign policy, but also about immigration and language. And our success and our image as entrenched and hermetically sealed in our culture, has set off a backlash; but it hasn't detained the momentum.

With every migration, the flame of the *cubania* is rekindled; the conjured Havana is made fresh once again. The flame often fuels as intense limbo. There have been great strides in and out of the community. But there also have been failures: mud trekked in the Everglades by weekend commandos on futile missions, hot air that rarely leaves the confines of little Havana. From the outside, the image is usually of the ferocious exiles who think the same, blinded by their anti-castrismo. But who are we?

We are a population so deeply rooted in Miami we seem entrenched in the city's character. Yet, and this is the great irony, we are a people who, in a flash, had to leave our mothers and fathers, children, sisters, and brothers and start all over again. We are daughters and sons who said good-bye, see you next week, and then didn't see their parents again for 25 years.

I think the better questions are these: What will there be once Fidel falls? What will there be in Cuba? What will there be in Miami? We will be exile no more, simply the protagonists of a particular capsule in time, a village of tiny lights, distant but no longer displaced.

4

Donde los Fantasmas Bailan Guaguancó: Where Ghosts Dance el Guaguancó

María de los Angeles Torres

El Amanecer en La Habana (Sunrise in Havana)

THIRTY days after my sixth birthday, my parents put me aboard a plane going from Havana, Cuba, to the United States. The classified U.S. government Operation Pedro Pan had procured visa waivers for children whose parents feared losing them to the communist state. I was one of 14,000 children sent unaccompanied. We were to have gone back to Cuba within months; instead, my parents and two sisters joined me in the United States, also intending eventually to return; but in 1961, the Cuban government decreed that if a person did not return within the sixty days allotted in the exit permit, the leave was considered a "definitive abandonment," and the Ministry of the Interior could confiscate his or her property. Such persons could no longer return to the island, even for visits; in effect, they were exiled. One year later, after the October Missile Crisis, the United States banned travel to Cuba. Thus, our return to the island was prohibited by both our home and host countries.

Still, ever since the day I arrived alone in Miami—July 30, 1961— I have been returning periodically to Cuba. I have forgotten most of the flights because they didn't really happen; I imagined them, over and over again. Most of my real flights were only 45 minutes long, yet these I recall with chilling detail: the turbulence that rocked the ten-passenger propeller plane during *un cicloncito;* the warm orange juice and cold sandwiches served on the short-lived New York-Havana flights; the small blond roaches on Pakistani charter planes from Miami on my oldest daughter's first visit to the island. What I remember most, however, is the arrival: the first glimpses of translucent aqua water, palm trees, and red dirt; the airport and the sour-faced immigration officials; the humidity; and the long, sticky ride to Havana. This is also what I remember most of my first trip to the United States, the departure, only in reverse order.

My need to return home remains intense, so powerful that I have passed it on to my daughters, Alejandra (born February 3, 1986) and Paola (October 20, 1989), who, although born in Chicago, are the ones who insist we return yearly. Only now, for the first time since my initial return, I no longer need to physically recover every inch of that beautiful island in the Caribbean that even today I call home. Still, I am in love with an island—its mountains, its waters, its buildings, its soil.

My love for the island is physical. The rhythm of people walking on the streets makes my body move differently; softer, much looser, particularly at the hips. The humidity alters the texture of my hair. The sun bronzes my skin. And the breeze caresses me gently as my parents caressed me, as I caress my daughters, as my husband and I caress each other today. I feel for physical spaces. Many of my most pleasurable and painful memories are located in geography: Contentment resides on the sands of warm beaches that I bathed in as a child; sadness lingers on the steps of my deck in Chicago where one hot summer evening as mosquitoes hatched I learned of the death of a friend. My passion for Cuba has been such that on my visits I could not sleep. I needed to soak in every second, always fearing that this might be the last return. Usually, exhaustion set in about five o'clock in the morning, and I would miss the sunrise.

On a trip to the island in 1995, however, I knew things had changed. That summer, in response to burgeoning debate on identity in which the exile community was proving itself more open-minded than officials in Havana, the Ministry of the Interior's *Centro de Estudios de Alternativas Políticas (CEAP)* and *the Unión de Escritores y Artistas Cubanos (UNEAC)*[1] organized a conference on Cuban identity. To demonstrate that they too were willing to speak to critics, a select group of academics, artists, and writers who had left Cuba were invited. I was among them. My departure was safely distanced more than three decades into the past; the government still refused to speak to those who left only recently. For a year and a half I had been unable to go to Cuba; I was refused a reentry permit after writing an essay for the *Miami Herald*[2] critical of Cuban policies toward its "communities abroad" (*la comunidad en el exterior,* or COCUEX, in bureaucrat-ese). Now we were being used in a war of images, and we knew it. Yet this was the only way we could return.

After two days at the rundown Habana Libre Hotel (formerly the Havana Hilton) where we were lodged for the conference, Nereida, Achy (a longtime friend on her first return trip), and I moved to an apartment in El Vadado. A friend who went into exile a few years earlier had loaned us her keys. Although her mother, a Dominican, came periodically and stayed there, the sixth-floor apartment was virtually unused. The art nouveau 1950s style furniture, which gives Havana homes a feel that is simultaneously dated and chic, was exactly as she left it. The plants were alive, thanks to neighbors who watered them. Books covered with a thin veil of dust lined the walls. The drawing table in the room in which I slept looked as though it were awaiting her return. Staying there reminded me of the painful losses that exile brings to those who leave as well as to those who stay. Yet despite this I was calm on this trip. Most nights I was able to sleep when I felt tired. From the balcony of the apartment, I saw a royal palm tree, parts of El Vadado, and *el malecón,* the Havana seawall. And it was from here that, after the first good night's sleep in my many returns, I watched the sunrise in Havana.

Recordándome Recordar (Reminders to Remember)

Growing up in the United States in the 1960s, my mother's insistence that we remember had provided the sustained connection to the island. She left behind a very close-knit extended family that had raised her after her own mother's death. My mother was born in Meneses, a small rural town consisting of one main street, in

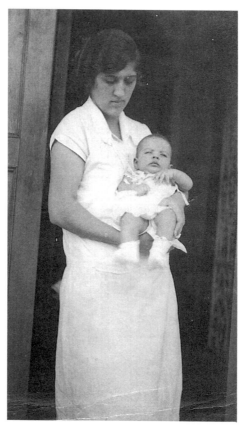

Illustration 4.1. *María de los Angeles Delgado (grandmother) and Maria Isabel Vigil (mother) in Meneses, 1926*

Villa Clara, a province in central Cuba populated mostly by Delgados, who had settled there from the Canary Islands some seven generations ago. Her mother, María de los Angeles Delgado Delgado, was one of seven children born to María Delgado and her husband and first cousin, Francisco Delgado. Marriage between first cousins was common in our family. By all accounts, she was the liveliest and most engaging of the children. She could outshoot and outride her brothers and sisters. She was also very caring: *Guajiros* still living in the area recalled that Cuca, as she was called, taught them to read and write. At sixteen, she married my grandfather, José Manuel Vigil Soler, who was born and raised in a slightly bigger town, Yaguajay, about fifteen miles from Meneses.

Unlike my grandmother's rural aristocratic background, my grandfather came from a family of tailors. Although born in Asturias, Spain, my great-grandfather had fought against the Spaniards. His "treason" affected his livelihood: his hands were severely crippled by Spanish soldiers who arrested and tortured him. His wife, Isabel Soler Pérez, was the matriarch who presided over the family with an iron fist. She made sure that all her children received a formal education. My grandfather, the oldest, became a doctor and through his work helped pay for his siblings' schooling. It was in caring for one of his patients that his young wife, at age 33, contracted poliomyelitis and died.

My mother was very close to the cousins on her mother's side, but she was cared for by my grandfather's sisters: Solita, a seamstress; Olga and Rosa, schoolteachers; and Alicia, a bookkeeper. It was in their home that we celebrated Christmas each year, and my great grandmother directed the holiday events from her white wicker rocking chair. The wooden house had an enormous front porch where my great aunts gathered to chat, smoke cigarettes, and pluck their eyebrows. They were continually fighting a losing battle against *hollín,* a thin black soot spewed from the sugar refineries around town. Inside the house, each bedroom had a towering, standing cedar closet. I would spend afternoons rummag-

Illustration 4.2. Jose Manuel Vigil and Maria Isabel Vigil in Meneses, 1927

ing through them, opening boxes of photographs and jewelry. At night I would sleep at Tía Solita's. She was the only sister who married and thus lived in a separate house two doors down from the main house. Solita's house was filled with threads of every imaginable color and buttons in odd shapes that she made and sold to other seamstresses. At night I would fall asleep in her bed, listening to the rhythmic songs of frogs and crickets.

My mother, María Isabel, was the oldest of two children, and despite her father's fierce objections, she became a chemist and went on to teach at the university. He wanted her to study pharmacology and take over her uncle's pharmacy in Yaguajay. Through Panchón, a cousin, she met my father, Alberto Torres Domínguez, from Matanzas, a medical student in Havana. A few years later they married and moved into a house in la Víbora, a middle-class neighborhood in Havana. This was my home in Cuba: a split-level with a garage on the ground floor and a small garden with an *areca* and red poinsettias that bloomed each Christmas. Red-tiled steps led to a balcony and the front door; inside were a living room and dining room, two bedrooms connected by a bathroom, and a kitchen. In back was a small concrete patio where my sister Alicia and I would play. It was here that, in preparation for a summer carnival, I learned to dance *el guaguancó*.

Despite her training and devotion to the sciences, my mother relished philosophy, literature, and art. She loved reading the mystic, Santa Teresa de Avila, who in her day had shocked her superiors by proposing that one could come to experience God through personal mystical connection, bypassing the patriarchal hierarchy of the Church. Her favorite poet was Gertrudis Gómez de Avellanedae, whose verse she would have us write and memorize on those short winter days in Cleveland, where we relocated after a year in Miami.

My mother was also passionate about Cuba. It was as if she had genetically inherited her grandfather's patriotism. One day I came home from school (we had moved to Texas by this time) and told her that I learned about the Spanish-American War. *"¿Qué se creen estos americanos?"* she asked. (What do these Americans think?) *"Eso no fue su guerra, eso fue nuestra guerra de independencia."* (That was not their war; that was our war of independence.) And when she was watching Hollywood movies such as "You are Always in My Heart," she would proudly claim, *"Un cubano compuso la música."* (A Cuban composed the music.) Years later, on a return trip to Cuba, I found her crying in her hotel room in Havana. She had just returned from a walk along Miramar's rocky beaches. *"Tú y tus hermanas piensan que lo único que perdí fue mi familia. Pero yo también deje este cielo, el malecón, esta tierra,"* she explained. (You and your sisters think that I only lost my family, but I also left behind this sky, el malecón, this land.)

My mother kept our Cuban history alive (later she blamed herself for instilling this obsession in her daughters and feared that she had abetted our return to Cuba), and my father gave us the gift of music. He was a talented musician who could have had a career in opera. His mother, already widowed when he was eight years old, remembered hunger from the lean years of *el Machadato* and made him study medicine rather than pursue his passion. Like everyone who left Cuba at the beginning of the revolution, my parents were allowed only one piece of luggage. My mother chose to fill hers with photographs and my father, his records. That's how we came to have scratched copies of the *"Orquesta Aragón," "los Chavales de España,"* and even the soundtrack of "South Pacific" in our family record collection. On later trips to Miami we had occasion to expand my father's collection with memorable music like *"Así cantaba Cuba"* and Ernesto Lecuona's U.S. recordings. His four daughters—my sisters and I, the youngest born in Texas—soon also discovered the pleasure of resurrecting other sensory memories, like *aguas de violetas,* an after-bath splash cologne used for babies and now only manufactured in Miami. Our family music and art were permeated with nostalgia. Like other Cuban families we had one of Félix Ramos' lush and colorful *framboyanes* (a land of tropical mimosa trees) hanging in our living room, alongside the over-reproduced 1950s iconographic photo of *el malecón.*

It was my mother who insisted we take Spanish lessons. Our practice was to sit at the kitchen table and write letters to her aunts in Cuba. We'd place the letters in air mail envelopes that we would stuff carefully with family photos and pieces of thread, needles, and razor blades—scarce commodities in Cuba in the late 1960s. Thirty years later, rummaging through one of the cedar closets in my aunts' home in Yaguajay, I found the photographs, a visual documentary of the evolution of our lives in the United States. Although far away, we existed in the present for them. With rare exceptions, the sole images that we had of our aunts were in the past. Indeed, our relationship to Cuba could only be with the past. Cuba had always been a memory; it didn't exist outside the horror stories we heard from relatives. Family memories increasingly were not of the island, but of exile. Thus our nostalgia was constricted by the impossibility of return and consequently became frozen in the past: *la cultura conjelada*.

Precisely *because* we were prohibited from returning to the island, our nostalgia was also a means of defying the official Cuban position that we were no longer Cuban. It bonded us to a past that defined who and why we were and what we had lost. Our nostalgia was a ritual of public mourning. Not part of the United States or of the island, our community's identity turned inward.

In some ways, though, my family didn't fit into the official exile community. We lived in Texas, unprotected by the exile enclave, and thus we were victims of racism. This led me to seek refuge in the civil rights movement. My politics, derived from my experiences in the United States, widened the growing wedge between my parents and me, particularly my father. My refusal to accept his characterization of Franklin Delano Roosevelt and Martin Luther King, Jr., as communists led to a long silent treatment. I also opposed the war in Vietnam. The schism of the Cold War continued to divide our family even further.

The differences on issues such as civil rights and the war inevitably led to reevaluating the Cuban revolution. Cuba had started to come into my life through the Chicano movement. Although initially I was shocked to see posters of Ché Guevara hanging in the United Farmworkers' offices, I came to see parallels between struggles for justice in the United States and other Latin American nations and the revolution in Cuba. When Salvador Allende was overthrown by Augusto Pinochet in 1973, the likenesses grew much clearer. In fact, it was through Chilean exiles that I first came upon *La Nueva Trova,* a new movement in Cuban music. The long-familiar bond of music was now fortified with songs from and about contemporary Cuba.

To actually engage with the island, however, would be to defy a principle that held family mythology in place. Moreover, new Cuba was taboo not only for my family, but for the United States as well. It was still illegal to travel to Cuba, as it was to buy or sell Cuban products, including newspapers and records. Engagement with Cuba was thus an illicit affair. Yet copies of *Granmas* and *Bohemias* somehow found their way into the United States. Silvio Rodríguez and Pablo Milane's records circulated as well. And then there were the poetry books, which smelled of the musty tropics and held words that, like my mother's family and history lessons and my father's songs, reminded me to remember.

El Nacimiento de una Ilusión (The Birth of an Illusion)

> *Illusions need not be false, that is to say,*
> *unrealizable or in contradiction to reality.*
> —SIGMUND FREUD, *THE FUTURE OF AN ILLUSION*

At first, the thought of actually returning to Cuba was so remote that it didn't seem possible. People were only leaving the island and coming to the United States, not returning. But then I began to meet North Americans who had traveled to Cuba. Instead of being helpful, however, they were obstacles to my own return. By then, Cuba and its revolution had assumed mythical proportions among various progressive movements in the United States. It was David versus Goliath. Cuba was the utopian ideal of the twentieth century; the entire Latin American Left was inspired by the Cuban revolutionaries who stood up to the Yankee imperialist. Cuba's exile community, on the other hand, was notorious for its support of reactionaries such as Richard Nixon. The political options were clearly demarcated along the fault lines of the Cold War.

In the early 1970s, debate ensued as to whether Cuban exiles should engage in Dialog with the government from which many of them had fled. Two groups led the discussion: radical Catholics, organized by the *Instituto de Estudios Cubanos,* and young exiles in search of identity and alternative politics. Increasingly the community's young exiles had begun to choose the side of the Cuban revolution. Lourdes Casal, a sociologist and poet, forged a link between the two groups and built the bridge that would finally allow our return to Cuba. Our visits were met with stiff opposition from our parents and the larger exile community. We were returning to the place from which our parents escaped. We were openly endorsing the system that disrupted their lives and foreclosed the futures they had envisioned. We were giving ourselves to the man who had betrayed them and their nation.

These clashes, which cut sharply along generational lines, were especially violent because they unfolded amid a cultural revolution in the United States that legitimized the struggle of children against their parents. Our parents wanted us to follow "Cuban ways," but on the other hand, they opposed our desire to return to Cuba. In contrast, we had adopted a U.S. ideology of parental defiance, here manifested by our travel to Cuba. Interestingly, instead of Americanization leading us farther from the homeland, it was the conceptual vehicle by which we returned "home."

The Cuban government reacted negatively to our desire to return as well. Officials feared that returning visitors might be infiltrators or could be used by the exile opposition to gather information about contemporary life on the island. They were also wary of our potential impact on the Cubans who remained on the island. After all, we lived in the country of the enemy. But we were insistent; we lobbied Cuban government officials at the United Nations and in other countries. Eventually, the Cuban government authorized the visit of a select number of exiles. Only two or three individuals, usually from different organizations, were allowed to enter at any one time. They were told by government officials not to tell anyone that they were Cuban. Official policy, after all, defined all who had left as traitors.

The news of these visits trickled through the island and the American Left. In 1977, the Cuban government granted the *Areíto* group fifty-five reentry permits. I was invited to return on this trip but declined, rationalizing this by telling myself that my political work was now in the United States. In reality, I feared a con-

La Brigada Antonio Maceo es una organizacion de jovenes cubanos fuera de Cuba que favorece el fin de bloqueo norteamericano hacia Cuba asi como la normalizacion de relaciones entre ambos paises. Apoyamos tambien el derecho de cada cubano de conocer mas de cerca la realidad actual de su pais de origen.

Me gustaria recibir una solicitud para participar en la Brigada Antonio Maceo:

Nombre _____

Direccion _____

_____

Brigada Antonio Maceo, P.O. Box 1125, Cathedral Station, New York, N.Y. 10025.

Illustration 4.3. Antonio Maceo Brigade leaflet

frontation with my parents, one that might lead to a definitive break.

A few weeks later, I read the group's account of the trip: "The name of Antonio Maceo, the mulatto general of the War of Independence, was chosen [as the namesake of the *Areito* group] because of our desire to maintain a continuity with the history of our homeland . . . our rebellion against the foreign decisions and against the historical circumstances which uprooted us from our homeland . . . and our protests against the blockade which impedes our need to get to know the Cuban reality."[3] Above all, the *Antonio Maceo Brigade* defended "the right of all Cubans to travel to Cuba to become reacquainted with the new Cuba and define their relationship to the homeland." I cried. The goals of the Brigade resonated deep into my past: to recapture for the nation all the children who had been taken away by their parents.[4]

I cried still more watching *55 Hermanos*[5] the documentary film that recorded the group's visit. It chronicled a meeting between Armando Hart, who was visibly moved as he spoke of his nephews who were sent to the United States, and Andrés Gómez, a Brigade member from Miami, who asked whether he and others could return to the island—not just for a visit, but to live. Indeed, many wanted to return. The answer to this plea for repatriation ultimately came from Fidel Castro, who told the young Cuban exiles that the country would be better served if they returned to their host country communities and worked there on behalf of the revolution. If the children of Operation Pedro Pan had shown the world the desperation of parents living under communism, the Brigade could testify to the horrors of capitalism and the exile community and life in the United States.

At the time, my sister and I were living in Austin, meeting and organizing other young exiles. In autumn 1978 we were invited as Brigade members to a meeting in Havana in which the Cuban government was to sign the accord of its Dialog with the community. This would be our first return. We had to be issued special reentry permits, because our parents refused to give us the original Cuba passports necessary to apply for new ones. What seemed to us a logical development in our lives—returning home—was to them an act of betrayal. We considered ourselves Cubans, entitled to return and even to participate within Cuban society. During the three-day meetings in Havana, Brigade members met and presented the Cuban government with our demands: a right to participate in island organizations, including the military; an institute to tend to the needs of those living abroad; and finally, repatriation.

The need to return was powerful. It was the solution to the incoherence we all felt, to the tremendous sense of loss that haunted our memories. The Antonio Maceo Brigade sprouted. In less than a year, eight chapters were organized. I joined the National Committee in the spring of 1979 while the Brigade was in the midst of defining itself and organizing the second travel contingent. We were a tightly knit group, nurtured, after all, by the community we were building, a community that we did not have with other exiles, in the broader U.S. society or in the American Left, which to this day discriminates against Cuban exiles. We believed our island "hosts," *compañeros,* who convinced us softly that it was our duty to serve *la patria* abroad, in the heart of the Cuban community. Thus we willingly accepted our host's directions, although our vision of who we were, our political role, and how to carry out that role were quite different. We wanted an organization that represented the aspirations of the Cuban community, or at minimum, advocated a normal relationship to the homeland, a desire we felt was legitimate. They wanted us to confront the community abroad. They wanted us to cut our ties with other progressive movements. They wanted us to concentrate on supporting Cuba.

We disagreed most strongly over how to organize the Brigade trips. For example, we urged more free time for the contingent so that people could reconnect with their families, but this was precisely what Cuban security forces did not want. Family visits were a sign of ideological weakness and were dangerous, particularly if the families were not "integrated." As I learned later, it was much harder to keep tabs on us if we had *tiempo libre* instead of programmed time. On one trip we were taken directly from the airport to el Campamento Julio Antonio Mella, the campgrounds in Bauta, about thirty minutes from Havana, where we stayed. There was only one phone; the lines formed immediately. This was the first return for most of the Brigadistas. Our hosts were not interested in facilitating personal contacts.

Another major battle revolved around the ideological purity of those returning for visits. The Cuban government insisted that we bring only those who clearly supported the revolution, a criterion used by the Venceremos Brigade, an organization of non-Cubans. We asserted, however, that no one, particularly Cuban exiles, could be in favor of something they did not know, and that the contingent must be open to all. The strongest advocate of this position was Carlos Muñiz, a 26- year-old Cuban who had been raised and was living in Puerto Rico. On April 26, 1979, months before the second contingent was to arrive in Cuba, Carlos was shot to death. *Omega 7,* a U.S.–based anti-Castro organization, took credit for the shooting. Although there were prior bombings, this event marked a declaration of war. Security concerns changed the way we organized and conceived our political work. We became much more like our island hosts, secretive and paranoid. Carlos' death drove us underground. We started to perceive our island hosts as people who cared for us and our security. In contrast, the FBI would not even investigate the murder because Puerto Rico was "out of its jurisdiction." We grew willing to help the Cuban government fight against the *contrarevolucion;* that now was our fight as well. Hence, despite the terrorism, over 200 young Cuban exiles traveled to Cuba with the second contingent of the Antonio Maceo Brigade, attesting to the strength of the illusion of going home and of becoming part of the nation.

Asuntos del Corazón y del Alma (Matters of the Heart and Soul)

The homecomings were intense. We had a sense of mission and community that bonded our generation in a very special way. We

Comunidad cubana condena el asesinato
Nueva etapa del terrorismo: acabar con el
Diálogo. / Me acuerdo de Carlos...

BARAGUA

PERIÓDICO DE LA BRIGADA ANTONIO MACEO   VOL. 1 NO. 2   JUNIO DE 1979 25¢

Foto por Maritta Lejeac

TERRORISTAS ASESINAN A CARLOS MUÑIZ VARELA

Miembro de la Brigada Antonio Maceo

El sabado 28 de abril en horas del anochecer, Carlos Muñiz Varela, 26 años, miembro de la Brigada Antonio Maceo fue asesinado en las calles de Puerto Rico. Era también presidente de la agencia que organiza viajes de cubanos residentes en Puerto Rico a Cuba, Viajes Varadero.

A una cuadra de la casa de su mamá; a donde se dirigía en su auto fue alcanzado por las balas provenientes de otro automóbil identificado por varios testigos como un Cutlass o Cougar. Los informes coincidieron en señalar a los ocupantes del auto agresor como tres hombres jóvenes, quienes dispararon entre 7 y 9 balas contra Carlos. Una de las balas atravezó su cabeza causando daño cerebral masivo y después de un dia de agonía, su muerte.

Carlos era un hombre de familia padre de dos niños.

La organización terrorista Comando O se responsabilizó por el vil asesinato.

Illustration 4.4. Baragua, newspaper of the Antonio Maceo Brigade

met Cuban exiles from Spain, Venezuela, Mexico, and all parts of the United States. We were a political phenomenon, children of the exile returning home.

Despite the tight programming, there was time to drink, to dance, to talk. We were insatiable. There was so much to recoup. It was in one of the late night *tertulias* in Pinar del Río that I met Nereida and Gilbert. They were sitting at the pool talking about literature and poetry and the songs of Silvio and Pablo. Cubans relish argument about everything; in this case, it was over whether Silvio or Pablo was the better musician or poet. I think we decided that Pablo was the better musician and Silvio the poet. Neri and I were to become good friends and Gilbert my first love in Cuba.

The need to have a human bridge, a shared sentiment that could sustain the closeness and regain our childhood, was great, and love flourished in the contingents. Men and women slept in different cabins, so Mango Lane, a long sidewalk of benches surrounded by mango trees, became our lovers' lane. Naturally we were oblivious to the policy directives that discouraged such relationships from developing. *"El grupo de atención"* was under strict orders to halt any relationships that began in the contingents. They were there to record and analyze who we were, to identify potential leaders, and to screen our ideological leanings. After all, we could be infiltrators; we could contaminate the youth. We would then return to our respective residences and dream about our next encounter. Often these did not happen, for our island lovers were warned that they would lose their jobs or Party standing if the relationship continued.

Surely we made a strong impact on our counterparts in Cuba as well. We were as rare for them as they for us, like a long-lost relative who suddenly appears in your life, bringing missing pieces of the family puzzle. Moreover, we were all living a utopian moment: Decidedly, we were on the side of justice, and even lovers could be sacrificed for the greater good. We eased our separations with Silvio's *"Como gasto papeles recordándote"* and Nazim Hikmet's *Duro Oficio el Exilio.* We also sponsored Cuban cultural events in the United States.

Illustration 4.5. Brigade Event, San Lucas Church, Chicago 1981 (author last on the right; photo by Gini Blaut-Sorrentini)

Fortunately, during the next decades, places did exist that would prove to be the real bridges to the island. One was the home of Eliseo Diego. Eliseo, a gentle poet with a wry sense of humor, engaged us. Unlike many who were suspicious of us, Eliseo and his family harbored us and nurtured us, although his children were undergoing a similar political transformation of their own. On free days, a group of us would walk from *Instituto Cubano de Amistad con los Pueblos* (ICAP)[6] headquarters to Eliseo's house in El Vadado, each carrying a bottle of Havana Club Añejo Rum. Usually Bella, Eliseo's wife, or Fefé, his daughter, would answer the door. Thus would begin the magical journey down the long hallway to Fefé's bedroom, which connected to the sitting area, where we would share and compare stories of growing up in Cuba and the United States. (Some of the parallels were amusing: For example, the exile community in the United States had branded The Beatles communists, whereas functionaries on the island opposed the band because they were imperialists.)

From these encounters grew shared points of reference that spanned geographical borders: the Sandinistas, members of Nicaragua's Sandonista National Liberation Front, had just defeated the dictator General Anastasio Somoza and young Cubans on the island, as well as those of us in the Brigade, were Sandinista supporters. The Cuban revolution, with its promise of equality and national sovereignty, bonded us to a worldwide movement for justice. Sometimes, late at night, Bella would take a head count for pillows and blankets. One by one we found corners in the house to sleep. Early the next morning we'd run across the empty rum bottles lined up in the hallway, making a *"cola"* of the evening's memories.

The returns to Cuba continued throughout the next few years, as did the visits to Eliseo's house. If there was only a free afternoon, I would visit him in his study. He would ask about our friends, and he would read his poems. Through Eliseo I began to love, not just long for, the intensity of the Cuban sunlight, the gentleness of the sea breeze, the parks of El Vadado. Eliseo had mastered the mystery of time, and he could slow its pace almost to a standstill. One hot night, as we sat on his porch a few hours before I was to leave, a family friend of Eliseo's came by. He had just returned from military tour in Angola. He was *"un internacionalista."* When Eliseo introduced me as a Cuban who lived in Chicago, he turned aggressive. "How could you be a Cuban and live in the United States?" I was devastated: for me, living in the United States was a sacrifice, a duty; for him, treason. I had never before seen Eliseo get upset, but now he defended me harshly. As I left for the airport, he hugged me and said, "Éste es tu país, vivas donde vivas, siempre eres Cubana." (This is your country, and you will always be Cuban regardless of where you live.)

Yet I still felt a distance between the Cuban part of me and my life in the United States. I had fallen in love with Matt Piers, a National Lawyer's Guild attorney who helped us in our anti-terrorist fight. Matt had never been to Cuba. In autumn 1982, Eliseo and Sara González, a member of La Nueva Trova, toured the United States. The Chicago chapter of the Brigade organized an event. Eliseo stayed in our home, and Matt and Eliseo took an instant liking to each other. Eliseo pronounced Matt one of the most civilized men he had ever met. He was infinitely grateful to Matt after the night of the event, when a group of angry exiles tried to disrupt the performance and Matt had to whisk Eliseo and Sara out the back door. On our first trip to Cuba, Eliseo was there for Matt. The next summer, Matt and I were married, and Eliseo became *el padrino de la boda.* "*El matrimonio,*" he wrote to us, "*significa el reconocimiento el misterio tremendo que es el encuentro del 'tú y yo' de hombre y mujer, a través de los abismos del tiempo y el azar.*" (The meaning of marriage is its recognition of the tremendous mystery of the encounter between "self and other" of man and woman, throughout the abysses of time and destiny.) Eliseo was not only a bridge to the island, he was a bridge to our hearts.

Two years later, I was pregnant. I wanted desperately to go to Cuba; I yearned for this connection for the life inside of me. But in response to the Reagan administration's launching of *Radio Martí,* a United States Information Agency program, the Cuban government canceled all trips by Cuban exiles, thus officially negating the accords of the Dialog. (Instead I reached out to Matt's past, and we traveled to Austria, the homeland of his parents. My child would be rich with heritages.) By the time my daughter, Alejandra, was born, state policy had changed once again, and the trips resumed.

We took our first trip to the island when she was two months old. Eliseo was suffering. His mother had died, and he was mourning. Another poet, Pablo Armando, and his family opened their home. His children, especially Teresa, Pablito, and Barbara, became like siblings, and his wife, Maruja, a friend. She even traveled to Chicago to help me during the birth of my second daughter, Paola. My Cuban life and my U.S. life had at last begun to merge, to hold a promise of coherence.

Illustration 4.6. Pablo Armando Fernandez and Paola Piers-Torres, Chicago, 1997 (photo by Patricia Boero)

La Muerte de una Ilusión (Death of an Illusion)

Although my increased trips to Cuba started to reveal a more realistic vision of how people really lived under Fidel, I still believed in the utopian ideal. The Reagan administration's brutal war on Central America served as the chilling reminder of what the alternative might be. The external threat on Cuba naturally offered a ready excuse to avoid addressing the island's internal problems. But little by little, the veil that hid the reality from the ideal started to tear.

I had been aiming to travel to Cuba with Alejandra at least once a year and in 1987, Matt accompanied us. We enjoyed a stay in Havana and then a week in Varadero with Barbara Fernández and a friend. That summer, Luis Orlando Domínguez, head of the Young Communist organization, was accused of corruption. Everyone in Cuba knew he was Fidel's protégée; in fact *Radio Bemba* (gossip), the most competent and up-to-date news source in Cuba, reported that

Fidel had known of Domínguez' private jets, luxury vacations, and lavish lifestyle but ignored it. Now it was Fidel who condemned him on national television before the trial began. But even this incident, a vivid example of the arbitrary and concentrated power in the hands of one man, failed to disillusion me.

During the summer of 1989 I was pregnant again, and Matt once again accompanied us to Cuba. The day we left for Havana, the *Miami Herald* reported that General Arnaldo Ochoa and several of his assistants had been arrested. Our friends cautioned us to be careful; something had happened—or was about to. Each night for the next six weeks, the government aired edited versions of the sentencing trial of Ochoa and fifteen officers from the Ministry of the Interior. There was a one-day delay in the broadcasts to facilitate editing by the Armed Forces. No one believed that Fidel was unaware of the alleged secret meetings with Colombian drug lord Pablo Escobar or the secret plans to develop a cocaine laboratory in Angola. And no one imagined that the defendants would be put to death. Following the broadcast was one of the numerous concerts that Pablo Milanés played throughout the island. How could two seemingly contradictory events—a grotesque Roman circus and a resounding expression of beauty—coexist?

We spent a few weeks on the beach and then traveled to Santa Clara to visit my mother's aunts. Little by little I forged a relationship with them, which I had failed to do during earlier visits. Matt departed, but I stayed on the rest of the summer with Alejandra at Pablo and Maruja's house. Perhaps I was in a state of heightened astuteness because I was pregnant; or maybe I sensed the very moment of rupture on the island. But something changed. The thin veil of illusion could no longer hide the ugly truth about Cuba: The revolution had engendered a grotesque, corrupt, tightly organized power formation. Ochoa and three other officers were sentenced to death.

Why had it taken me so long to understand? I had coupled my longing to return home with the utopian dream of a perfect society, forming an impenetrable, tightly woven illusion. The death of an illusion is painful. It challenges our beliefs and frustrates our need to believe. Its death is a realization that our deepest, most ancient wishes have gone unmet.[7] It leaves us powerless and vulnerable.

I did not want to sever my ties to the island. In the next few years, I continued to seek ways to continue connecting. I became a board member of the Cuban American Committee, a policy and research think tank. I was convinced that normalizing relations was not only the right policy for the United States, but that as a result, Cuba would inevitably have to normalize its relationship to the exile community. This would, by definition, engender change on the island. By now I had forged friendships with scholars, writers, and artists outside the security cordon that generally surrounded us. Despite warnings that I was endangering my reentry permits, I began inviting them to academic and cultural exchanges. I would take other academics and U.S. foundation officers to their homes. I was convinced that we could make a difference in Cuba. By including real academics rather than security officers parading as scholars, we could help more critical voices in Cuba to gain leverage on the internal debate.

Independent scholars were interested in retelling the history of the island to pick up missing pieces, including information about those who had left. U.S. Cubans wanted to expand the definition of "Cuban-ness" to include both the exile and the island. Our framework surpassed the political and geographical boundaries drawn by the revolution and the Cold War. The Berlin wall had fallen, and the economic crisis in Cuba accelerated. Surely change was around the corner. The need to return intensified, but the stakes now were much higher. I no longer believed in the illusion; rather I saw my role as one of promoting and facilitating real change in Cuba. In the eyes of the Cuban government, I was no longer a P.C. (persona confiable), but perhaps a collaborator with dissidents, if not quite yet a traitor. I no longer felt safe when I returned to Cuba. At one point I was threatened by the security officer in charge of the communities abroad, who reminded me that there were hospitals in Cuba for people who did not understand what dissidents were. This particular threat was made within the context of a meeting at which I was requesting permission for a friend in Miami, a spokesperson for one of the human rights groups on the island, to return to see his dying grandmother.

When I returned to Chicago, I would inevitably feel as though I hadn't done enough. I would start to plan for the next trip, always believing that if I just tried harder, I could make a difference. I didn't realize then that I was merely replaying my childhood. My daughter had just turned six, the age I had been when I was separated suddenly from my family. I was literally returning every three months. I felt that if I could somehow make it back, I could undo the journey that had cast me from the island. I nearly destroyed my marriage. Fortunately, we weathered the storm. And Eliseo and Pablo were there to support me.

Los Límites del Diálogo (The Limits to Dialog)

The wall between Havana and Miami gradually started to come down. Colleagues and friends began to leave the island. Some moved to Mexico, others to Spain, some even to Miami. The circle outside of Cuba widened. Conversation intensified. Miami became not only a point of transfer, but also a site of curiosity and exploration. People felt they could say things publicly they could only say in their homes in Cuba. I began to understand the pain of exile, not only as my family drama tucked away somewhere in the distant past, but also as a living, open wound. I watched newly arrived friends struggle with the reality that they could not return to Cuba to see their families. Those of us who could go back provided a point of contact. The new exiles in turn offered insights into Cuba that we could only imagine. José and Ileana's house became the decompression chamber, a place somewhere between Havana and Miami where two halves of a whole that had been violently severed could once again reconnect. People could exchange those references previously denied them.

All of this contributed to a cultural renaissance of sorts in Miami and the emergence of art exhibits, plays, film festivals, neighborhood parties for island visitors and recently exiled friends, all fostered by a conscious effort to eliminate geography as the criteria by which people related to each other. The healing of *la nación cubana* was slowly but unmistakably occurring in exile. The exile community was changing in so many ways: A second generation had come of age whose voice was only now being heard, and its warm reception of *los recién llegados* sharply contrasted with the way *Marielitos* had been ostracized. Island visitors were welcomed openly, and island culture, like the music of Albita Rodríguez, consumed gratefully.

The paradigm of fixed geographical identities could no longer explain our reality, a reality now framed by points of reference from both the United States and Cuba. But the notion that Cuban culture, especially contemporary Cuban culture, could flourish in exile threatened the island government. A *Miami Herald* article written by Mirta Ojito entitled, "Miami, more Cuban than Havana?" was the final blow.[8] Government officials went on the offensive. They dusted off the covers of policies from the late 1970s and, with the same language that had emerged from the Brigade, reached out to the community. They resurrected Lourdes Casal by dedicating a conference on Cuban identity to her. Their manipulation was so obvious that they did not even bother to spell her name correctly. Furthermore, they claimed to be seeking reconciliation with those who had left, but recently departed exiles were not allowed to join in the discussion. How could they exclude recent exiles—many of our culture's most important artists and writers—from the debate? The battle was on, but so was the unveiling of the porous nature of geographical and political borders, so evident to me, particularly, from the vantage point of Miami.

The Cuban government further responded to its perceived threat by hosting a Dialog in the spring of 1994, fashioned along the lines of the 1978 Dialog, which was a conference on *"la nación y la emigración"* (the nation and its émigrés). I discuss the internal bureaucratic turf wars surrounding this conference in my essay in the *Miami Herald* of May 1, 1994. I was invited to attend, and although my critical position was widely known, I went nonetheless. I felt that I needed to bring closure to the official process in which I had been involved since the first Dialog. However, the manipulative underpinnings of the event were apparent early on: the term "emigrant" was used in lieu of "exile" in an attempt to repudiate the existence of exiles or political opposition of any sort. Key individuals in Cuba and from the exile community were not invited. Essential topics were excluded from the agenda. Conference decisions were made unilaterally.

The production of images became more important than the substance of the meetings. On the flight to Havana, for instance, we saw a video about the upcoming event, showing where we were to stay and convene. It was laced with nostalgic music, people-on-the-street views of the conference, and interviews with figures such as Monsignor Carlos Manuel de Céspedes, Bishop of Havana, and Elizardo Sánchez, a leading human rights activist, both voicing cautious support of the effort. Interestingly, although they could be featured in a Cuban television production about the conference, they were not invited to the conference itself.

Not surprisingly, the conference ended in a fiasco. A private reception with Fidel Castro was videotaped without the consent of the participants. Only 4 of us out of the 225 Dialog participants had chosen not to attend. It was not a planned boycott; it just happened. While we were sitting together at lunch, just after the reception announcement, Ruth Behar, Emilio Cueto, Nereida, and I said to each other, almost in unison, *"Yo no puedo ir"* (I can't go). The conference had been one of the crassest examples of the Cuban government's attempt to manipulate our legitimate desire to engage with the country of our birth. We couldn't bring ourselves to herald the event at a reception.

That night I met a friend at the lobby of El Hotel Nacional. We were comparing notes: She was covering the conference for a TV network, and I was to write an article for the *Miami Herald*. As we sat down to talk, she was approached by a young man from the Ministry of the Interior who offered to sell her a copy of the videotape of the reception. The guests hadn't even had time to return to their hotels, and their images were being peddled to the international media without their knowledge. The next day at the airport, I encountered another friend, who had also been on the National Committee of the Antonio Maceo Brigade. When I reported the videotape incident to her, she responded angrily, "That's a lie!" By the time we arrived in Miami, however, the video was being aired on all the TV stations. She later called to apologize. "I just couldn't imagine that they could ever do something like that." The video seriously damaged the credibility of many of the reformers involved in the process, because it showed them praising and flirting with Castro.

We had left for Havana the week before the conference from the Miami airport without incident, a sign that the intransigent forces of the exiles were in decline. Liz Balmaseda and I had sat at St. Michel's bar in Coral Gables, contrasting the difference in atmosphere between the first Dialog in 1978, when bomb threats had forced us to fly out of Atlanta, to the current civility, which allowed for fundamental disagreements to be aired publicly without violence. For me, these events called into question the strategy of Dialog with government officials. It convinced me that I was on a collision course with the Cuban government: I supported lifting the U.S. embargo; they did not. The *Miami Herald* article would be my public break with the island's official world, and in particular, with the government officials who handled the Cuban community project.

I felt saddened and liberated at the same time. I knew that reconciliation was still the right position, as it had been when I first returned to Cuba. Yet I was powerless to do anything about it through official channels. The ties had to be forged outside the official world. There were my great aunts, my friends, and my past. I felt free of the Cold War blinders that had made consistent and coherent positions difficult to attain much less express. This was both liberating and personally healing. I called my mother and told her that I understood why she had left Cuba.

My daughters and I spent that summer in Miami instead of traveling to Havana. My healing process was also bringing me closer to Matt. I felt that he was helping me build bridges, facilitating my travels so that the girls could connect with their multiple heritages. I felt safe in our marriage. I realized that I could love him without losing myself.

Aceptando Exilio (Accepting Exile)

Years earlier in Cuba, Maruga, a close friend who lived in Varadero, had introduced me to the publishers of *Vigía,* a handmade journal compiled by artists and writers in Matanzas. *Vigía* was special. It was the first island publication to include works by poets who had left the island. Eliseo adored them and asked us to help out if we could. What resources we could we sent their way. For several years many of us regularly made the pilgrimage from Havana to Matanzas to visit them. The afternoons spent at *Vigía* were magical; light reflected on the walls in a spectrum of colors as the sun shone through blue-paned windows. Young women, men, and children sat around a table as if rolling tobacco, telling stories as they hand-assembled each magazine. And most important, Matanzas was my father's city. My trips to visit *Vigía* gave me glimpses of where my father had been born and raised.

In the winter of 1995, the publishers invited me and other exiles to attend the tenth anniversary of *Vigía,* but I had been, in effect, banished from the island for a year. At that time we needed permission from two governments to travel to the island. After some prodding the U.S. Treasury Department issued a permit, but Cuba's government would not. In the meantime anti-immigrant sentiment ran high in the United States. Cuban refugees became a flashpoint in the Florida governor's race. Bill Clinton, who had lost the gubernatorial re-election in Arkansas during the Mariel refugee crisis, reversed a long-standing policy of welcoming Cuban refugees and ordered the Coast Guard to intercept rafters at sea and deport them to Cuba. We were again being shunned by two states. The Cuban exile community was in shock. Although the *raison d'etrê* for exile had not changed—in fact repression was likely to increase—the special place that Cuban exiles inhabited in the symbolism of U.S. policy had lost its political capital. When the United States was at war with the former Soviet Union, refugees coming into the country demonstrated to the world that this system was better than the other one. Why hadn't the exile community realized that it was being used?

Those of us raised outside Miami had felt this long ago, but to talk about xenophobia or discrimination against Cubans was heresy. The world of those in the battle zone of the Cold War was one-dimensional: Everything was either/or; you loved or hated Castro and conversely, the United States. Any deviation from this simplistic formula left one vulnerable to accusations of treason. Voicing support for the civil rights movement, for example, sparked accusations of crossing over to the other side of the great ideological fault line between capitalism and communism.

Likewise, to criticize the Cuban government was to become a *gusana*. For instance, I was dining at a friend's home days after the Cuban government shot down one of the planes of *Hermanos del Rescate,* killing two pilots. Unlike other traditional exile organizations, *Hermanos del Rescate* succeeded in establishing a following on both sides of the Florida Straits. By spotting *balseros* and alerting the Coast Guard, they saved tens of thousands of lives. The organization had begun to escalate its activities, crossing international boundaries into Cuban territory and dropping leaflets from the planes. Surely this was civil disobedience, but still, did a government have the right to murder in cold blood?

My outrage prompted heated discussion. A former member of the Weathermen Underground defended the Cuban government. "After all," she said of the *Hermanos,* "they broke the law." For many sympathizers of the Cuban revolution, the right of protest was contingent on the content of protest. *Gusanos* were not to be granted the rights and privileges of protest that white, middle-class North Americans took for granted and, indeed, demanded for themselves.

In my professional world the double standard was also rampant when it came to Cuba, as was intolerance and even racism against those who criticize the Cuban government. We would never think of collaborating with the CIA on research, and in fact many of us protested their presence on college campuses. Yet exchanges in Cuba were controlled by one or another of the intelligence centers. Few protested, with the excuse that a young scholar once expressed to me: "If I say anything critical, it will jeopardize my chances of getting a visa, and then I can't do my research." Furthermore, progressive North Americans, already leery of immigrant involvement in homeland issues, are the first to dismiss Cuban exile criticism by questioning its legitimacy and even its genetic authenticity. A program officer at a major foundation once queried, in response to my criticism that exiles were excluded from many of the exchanges, "Why should you care so much about what happens on the island anyway? You're only half-Cuban, after all." The predicament of the half-breed, not entitled to a voice in either culture or state, persists. My migratory status and political views make me somehow less authentically Cuban: In her eyes, it took away *half* of my *Cubanness*.

Perhaps more unfortunate is that this unipolarity of political discourse has malformed both our politics and our vision of ourselves. We have failed to develop a coherent political discourse that is critical of both governments or that even views both governments as state actors, not allies. To pose a critical stance of both governments was not an option. To do so was to be unwelcome in home and host countries. I have now begun to shape my thinking along the contours of the diaspora experience. We seek a place, a home that cannot be fabricated within a singular locale, either U.S. or Cuban, but within both. We need to accept and act upon the multiplicity of places in which our identities have been constructed. Accepting our role as a diaspora community in the United States also demanded that we struggle for our rights here.

It meant disregarding our single-issue agenda (either to destroy or to support Castro) and developing one that encompassed immigrant and language rights, health care, and economic opportunity, alongside the call for a more open society in *both* our home and host countries. For me, it ultimately meant accepting, finally, that I was part of the exile community.

Donde los Fantasmas Bailan el Guaguancó

With the death of illusions, we come to accept who we are. I celebrated my fortieth birthday at Centro Vasco with Liz Balmaseda, who shared her window into the soul of Miami and whose courage to speak out made me realize that exile need not be accepted on the terms of those in power in Havana or Miami; Elly Chovel, who had introduced me to other Pedro Pans and helped me develop a sense of place within a generation; Joey Greer whose home I stayed at when I first arrived in Miami and with whom I now shared a progressive vision of politics; Ruth Behar, a friend and colleague who encouraged me to write of my experience in my own voice; and of course Nereida, with whom I shared the journey back to exile. Candy Sosa played and sang "Yolanda," a Pablo Milanés song, right there on *la Calle Ocho*.

The journey that began with my lonely flight to the United States, which continued through many legs of return to the island in an effort to undo my fate, now reached its end in the place I had most wanted to avoid: Miami. *I was a Cuban exile.* I shared a history with other Pedro Pans, with Cubans raised in the United States, with friends just arriving in Miami, with friends still on the island. To acknowledge this did not mean I had to deny the pain of exile or to accept its most reactionary politics; nor did it mean that I had to denounce the island. Indeed, I am fortunate to have the contemporary island as an integral part of who I am, despite the manipulation of the Cuban state.

That autumn, I spent three months in Spain with my family and students. That vantage point allowed me to see my identity as a product of the Americas, north and south. I had always fought against living in Chicago, but this new distance made me realize that I could enjoy and thrive in that city. Little by little I began to take pleasure in who I am, in my daughters, in my marriage. The need to love and be loved is quite powerful; the fear that we could lose that love can compel us to do things that deny us the very possibility of love. Returning home to Cuba had been my way of recovering what had been lost, but it had also become a way for me to deny myself the possibility of real love in the present. Perhaps I was afraid that I would lose that as well.

Now I had to come to terms with my past. On my trip to the island in the summer of 1995, I had begun that process, although I was not fully aware of its implications until a year later. Meaning often sets in after reflection, which by definition needs distance. This trip was so different from earlier returns. It was my first visit to the island without Eliseo, who had died in Mexico the year before. Emptiness engulfed me. I had pushed all the buttons, and I did not feel as though I might leave something behind that I could not regain. It was all part of me now: the music played by Sara González and Marta Valdez; my friends at *Vigía;* the warmth of the waters at Varadero; the affection of my second family, la familia Fernández. As on other trips, I felt that this could be the last one, although something inside me was at peace with this possibility. I had, after all, watched the sunrise.

I decided to visit the house where I lived as a child. I had often driven past the house in Havana, and each time I had the same sensation: I was shocked by how small it was. This sense repeated itself each time I returned, as if every time was the first time. The power of the childhood image prevailed. Yet I had not walked up the red-tiled steps to the balcony; I had not entered the house and stepped back to the concrete garden in which my sisters and I spent endless hours playing and dancing. I needed to confront my ghosts.

The same family who had been given the house after we left was still living there. Little had changed, including the furniture inside,

Illustrataion 4.7. Author on the patio in Havana, 1958

except for a tall apartment building under construction in what was the empty lot where my sister and I imagined a grazing field filled with white, wild horses. The sunlight would be blocked, the owner complained. Standing on the concrete porch, I wanted to recapture for my mother the spiritual things she had lost and to tell her that I finally understood her decision to send me to the United States, that I could empathize with the fear she must have felt. I wanted my father to understand why I needed to return. I wanted to share this moment with my daughters; they would be amused by this glimpse of their mother's childhood. I wanted Matt with me.

During the next year, I came to understand that I had not lost my Cuban past; it was with me regardless of where I resided physically. It was my past, rooted in over five generations of relatives buried on that beautiful island in the Caribbean. I also came to accept that I could not change that past, it was as it was. The heritage, the memories, the fate. I did not have to forfeit my link to the past to become one with my present. I merely had to find a peaceful place where I could enjoy my memories. And where my ghosts could once again dance *el guaguancó*.

Notes

1. UNEAC, La Unión de Escritores y Artistas Cubanos, is a government-controlled union of writers and artists.

2. Torres, María de los Angeles. 1994. "Exiles as pawns," *Miami Herald*, May 1, p.1.

3. *Areíto, Número Especial, Spring 1978, pp. 4–5.*

4. The first Brigade contingent included several Cuban exiles living in Spain, Mexico, and Venezuela as well.

5. *55 Hermanos,* a documentary film directed by Jesús Díaz, was based on the Brigade's visit to Cuba. The visit had a profound impact on the island, and the film that chronicled the visit drew record crowds of viewers in Cuba. People exited movie theaters in tears. The island-based Casa de las Américas published the Brigade's story, *Contra viento y marea.* On subsequent trips to Cuba, Brigade members were stopped on the streets and embraced.

6. ICAP, or Instituto Cubano de Amistad con los Pueblos, was the organization in charge of our visit. Its employees' time cards, which hung on the wall of the garíta, or guard's post, listed *secreto as their occupation.*

7. Freud, Sigmund. 1961. *The Future of an Illusion. New York: Anchor Books.*

8. Ojito, Mirta. 1994. "Miami, more Cuban than Havana?" *The Miami Herald*, May 1. p.1.

5

Not the Golden Age
Nereida García-Ferraz

First Stage

THE FIRST thing was to sell the piano and replace it with one of lower quality, because the inventory wouldn't allow it to go missing. My father took care of that. I remember the original piano was a Kimball, and it was made in Chicago. That is why "Chicago" was one of the first words I learned to read. I would sit up on the bench, and there, while I spun around to adjust the seat to my height at the keyboard, I'd see the word "Chicago" on every spin, a curious thing for a six-year-old girl who lived in Guanabacoa.

Getting out of Cuba took many years. Mami packed us new suitcases every year because we always had to use our traveling clothes. It was the 1960s, and the atmosphere in the house was full of tension. I found refuge in the games I played with my cousins, in books, and in those Beatles songs that reached us. I remember that I learned to keep my eyes fixed on the landscape: I knew that one fine day I wouldn't be there any more, so I enjoyed it all in a very special way, as if to keep it from escaping my memory, to keep the archive of my mind from betraying me.

It was different at school: Much as I tried, I could never join anything. We were marked—my sister and I—as the *gusanas,* the worms, the ones who were leaving the country. There was no avoiding it.

The Photograph

My mother was always packing up, almost as far back as I can remember. She was always ready to travel. Where to? That always changed. It depended on dates, on reasons, on life itself. During one of her bouts of packing up not long ago (this time on her way to Miami), she spent a few days at my house, and with her came the packages with the family photo albums—four altogether. The thick red one holds the most important family images, the ones from the other side of the sea. The other albums, shabbier, snapshot-sized, keep our life in the United States in image form.

Naturally, it's always fascinating for me to pass the time imagining a full concert of images. In this way I've organized my head many times, visually ordering the map of my family life. The red album—the one I prefer—is fascinating. Faces appear in it that I no longer even remember: distant cousins, relatives of relatives, my grandparents as a young couple smiling from eight-by-tens taken in the city of Havana in the 1920s and 1930s. These are

Illustration 5.1. Mi Abuela (center), 1935

images that always make me nostalgic and bring to my mind *danzones* and fashions: Grandmother before she became my grandmother, active, and hardworking, together with her mother, brothers, sisters, and uncles; everyone in pale-colored, lightweight suits, posing casually; attractive young people, immigrants from an impoverished Spain, scrambling to make a better life.

Another photo I love is one of Grandmother in a dark hat with my mother and my uncle Manolo—still children—crossing a street in La Habana Vieja: my uncle, dressed in a sailor's suit and Mami, wearing a huge bow on her head and looking absent-minded and very girlish.

Some images have always spoken to me of my Grandmother Margarita's urban character, such as the pharmacy on Pepe Antonio Street in Guanabacoa, which they later had to sell when hard times fell during the Machado years, or a yellowing image of Mami on her fifteenth birthday, leaning against a column in a photographer's studio: discreet, elegant, unconscious of her fate, lost in that magic instant when light entered the dark enclosures of the camera. That image is fifty years old now.

These photographs, and others from the 1950s, have helped me to rebuild myself, to place pieces of the puzzle, searching always for that bigger image that will help me understand what paths everyone took to get to the places they are today. Or perhaps, to keep me busy and let me lose myself on those streets that now are a bit more mine, thanks to these familiar, well-studied pictures. For me, these photos have always revealed much more than simple emulsion on paper or the magic of a gaze fixed on the future. They have always, for some reason, come to frame my own surroundings. They bring the consolation of knowing that, at one time, my family lived whole eras in a single place, had belonged to a place: the island. And, perhaps, of whiling away an afternoon imagining what would have happened had history been different. Youth was, for them, truly valuable, tied to development: "We were so young," my elderly grandmother exclaimed whenever you mentioned the family album to her.

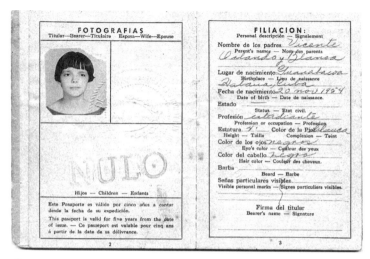

Illustration 5.2. Author's passport

These images, which I look at every so often always have the same effect on me: They evoke afternoons when, running to my cousin's house, I would hear, on someone's radio down the block, the mournful voice of Barbarito Diez. As a child, that music had a strange effect on me, like an enormous emptiness that I could never understand, like that Sunday afternoon light in Havana that grew longer and longer until it seemed that everything stood still inside you. I'd get rid of that sensation by throwing myself into other realities. I was well aware that one day I would leave the island, that everything would be different then, that I would live in another city, among other smells, beneath another light. That's how it was for several years, until we finally left.

Kodak

When the mailman brought us letters from the North, those red and blue envelopes carried a peculiar, delicate perfume: They smelled of gum, because they almost always contained a stick of

Juicy Fruit, cut in two, for my sister and for me. They also contained photos: small color photos of my aunt and uncle reclining
by an enormous late-model car or in front of some well-trimmed
garden, with my cousins dressed in a multitude of colors and
stripes and so on; they all looked different, everything from their
haircuts to their expressions had changed. That caused tremendous amusement in the family and comments such as, "They just
left yesterday and look how well they've done; they all look
younger." Obviously, they were referring to the prosperity and
rapid advancement of the ones who had left. Beneath that tropical
sun of ours, our own reality seemed to be in black and white. In
Cuba we hadn't seen anything new in years; on the contrary, our
chairs were breaking, the table limped a little, the Emerson television—a heavy, square, somber-colored box—could barely be seen
now, and when you could see it, you usually couldn't hear it, so it
was a rare day when the whole thing worked the way it should.

We didn't see our reality in the 1960s as a livable time but as an
interval, a measure waiting for the key moment: our departure.
We had no future on that island. We were growing up with a
strange sense of being set apart, of not completely belonging.
That's how it was until I was just about to turn fifteen: One month
before my birthday, in October 1971, when we got the visas for
our *definitive* departure.

Second Stage

> *The little circle of chance*
> *"...fell from the sky, didn't kiss the ground"*
> —NEREIDA GARCIA-FERRAZ

At the end of the 1970s I had my first exhibition. I remember I
was part of a feminist collective, and we organized a show; I had
two collages in it. The day of the reception a somewhat older
woman who was contemplating them called me over:

"You must be Cuban," she said, and smiled. "My name is Lourdes Casal."

We immediately became friends. She was going around giving lectures in the city, and I was still a student at the Art Institute of Chicago. The fact that she had recognized my Cubanness was very gratifying to me at that moment. I had spent years exchanging letters with my grandmother who had stayed in Cuba, and I explained to Lourdes how I wanted—or rather, needed—to return and visit the island. I felt such relief when I told her this; it was as if I could finally tell someone aloud what I had been repeating to myself for so long: "I want to go back to Cuba." And I was not afraid. I remember the enormous feeling of relief I felt when she told me that I wasn't the only one, that there were many young Cubans like me who had the same need to go.

Months later, without knowing exactly what to expect—and very nervous, of course—I packed a light suitcase for the trip back: I brought my camera and 20,000 questions and needs. I was going back with a brigade by the name of Antonio Maceo. I remember that when I told my mother, she burst out crying and begged me to take good care of myself.

In Havana everything hit me at once: a tremendous thunderstorm and the smell of the island. I didn't arrive with the group but a week later; it was the end of Carnival week, and a driver took me to El Vedado. I recall standing at the entrance to the Hotel Habana Libre and trying to reconstruct the way to get from there to Grandmother's house in La Lisa.

I took a full bus with a leaky roof and, barely able to see, got out at Avenue 51 right before the entrance to La Lisa, just past the bridge that separates that municipality from Marianao. I had to cross about eight blocks of a neighborhood I scarcely recognized: It was already dark, and my clothes clung to my body as I walked. At last I recognized my grandmother's house, even though the entranceway was unlit and the oleander and the snowdrop plant no longer grew in the garden. I opened the gate and, as if in a strange dream, knocked on the door of the family house. The blue glow of the TV set was all that lit the scene. Grandmother opened the door, and I think the surprise practically killed her when I told her who I was, her granddaughter, back from the North.

I wanted to take photos, lots of photos, and bring them back to show them to my mother, to show them here, to have them with me. We hadn't been able to take a single picture the first time, and now I was returning as a photographer. I wanted photos of everything. I didn't use a flash, and I used very long exposures to get a single image. From this trip I have a series of photos that I took of some of Grandmother's neighbors and more of the province of Oriente where we attended a meeting. This latter

*Illustration 5.3. Author's grandmother, 1979
(photo by author)*

series was very revealing to me: I identified with the little girl, the central character in a group of people from the countryside who didn't know what else to offer when they saw us. We were young, we came with thousands of questions, and we were leaving in a couple of weeks. So Roxana, who was a singer and came from Puerto Rico, began to sing, and the silence and the night became one. For me, this song was a perfect expression of how I felt. I wrote in my journal:

> *Viajo tu mirada*
> *Lo que oyes, tus manos*
> *Cierta claridad que caei entonces*
> *Con exactitud, en tu mirada*
> *Recreando un pedazo de historia*
> *La puerta que da vueltas*
> *Dulce cielo.*

> I travel your gaze
> your hearing, your hands,
> a bit of clarity falling then,
> with exactitude, in your memory
> recreating in a piece of history
> the door that revolves
> sweet heaven.

Third Stage

The revolving door of the Jose Martí Airport added another dimension to everything about being Cuban. I lived in the midst of contradictions, but I was also full of other, greater certainties. Each trip was different and at the same time equal to the one that preceded it. We'd make our preparations at my house in Chicago. The group would get together on the weekend: we'd brew coffee and hold intense conversations. The city filled with meaning: We met new Cubans, we spoke of our lives, of returning, of our experiences. We were each very different but we clung in a way to what

we had in common: being Cubans. We'd invite musicians and poets from the island and show Cuban films. We'd begun to turn
what had been seriously missing for too long into reality. Suddenly,
something new and important was happening. We were learning
and getting closer to our history. We would return to Cuba.

That's how it went for three or four years. I never got tired of it.
I drew and painted in the meantime. I thought it was really up to
our generation to "make a difference." I remember furiously defending, at the top of my voice, my right to travel, to think, to criticize, always from my own personal experience, in the place where
I was born. Traveling to Cuba became a necessity of the first order,
but the contingents and the Brigade began to appear very struc-
tured and limiting to me. I wanted my own time in Cuba. I needed
to sit in a park without feeling rushed, to find my own point of
view. I remember walking around La Habana Vieja one day, taking
photos of the street signs, the walls and bricks making delicate

*Illustration 5.4. Antonio Maceo Brigade, 1980 (photo courtesy of author, third
from the left).*

drawings, the textures, the patina of time. I found my own traces in those ruins. Once, one of the people who attended our group saw me taking those pictures and got very upset at my choice of photographic subject. According to him, I was looking for the ugliest side of the city instead of searching for "the smiling face of some Young Pioneer, something more positive about the Revolution." This, of course, disgusted me, but it did not cool my desire to keep photographing those walls. I did it for myself. With those fragments I was constructing my own little piece of the city. I photographed buildings, balconies, rooftop terraces, streets, parks, cemeteries. I cut loose from the group and made my own connections; I didn't want to have to state my reasons.

I began making good friends on the other side with those who shared these things with me. Some of us in the Brigade began to feel upset at all the structure, all the "youthful enthusiasm." Everybody didn't see things the same way, but that was precisely the most interesting thing. It was like finding one place inside of another, which in turn formed part of something even larger. I hadn't been such a young girl when I left Cuba, so from my first visit back I had a pretty clear idea of what was going on. I knew that there weren't many choices, and I thought it was essential to assume the differences, to exercise tolerance. I needed to get to know, to find myself.

I met marvelous people who welcomed me. I connected with my grandmother in a different way, almost like friends. There were no secrets between us; we laughed about everything. She was very good at reading cards. She had a kind of sixth sense: She always guessed right. Each symbol was like a door that opened or closed, depending on the designs of fate. I came and went. Came happy, went back sad. I started having trouble finding my place back here.

Around 1983, I was invited back for the tenth anniversary of the magazine *Areíto*. I was going for one week on my first trip without the Brigade. This trip was different. This time we stayed in a hotel, and the lectures and discussions were about Cuban culture. I felt freer, and one night I connected with a family that sort of became my own. I went back many times to that house on Calle 20. There I improvised an art studio in one bedroom and spent two months painting pictures for an exhibition that was to be held in the Galería de Plaza. There I met the painters of my generation, the poets, the critics. I sort of lived the life of Havana in the mid-1980s. It was the Havana of the Film Festivals: *La Opera del Malandro, Lejanía,* and *La Bella del Alhambra;* of rum swigged from the bottle; of theses at the University of Havana, at the School of Letters; of book parties at the Palacio del Segundo Cabo; of buying gasoline-rationing coupons on the black market. All that started to affect me. There was continuity from one visit to the next. But the exhibition never took place: It was canceled, because suddenly in 1985, a powerful radio station started broadcasting from the United States to the island. To make things worse, the station was called Radio José Martí.

The Cuban exile community was no longer welcome in Cuba. Unlike the children's magazine *La Edad de Oro,* which was once edited by Jose Marti, this new communications channel using his name did not herald a Golden Age.

I went back to Chicago with the work I had done in Havana. Making paintings in Cuba and not being able to exhibit them had shown me another impossibility: it was *here or there, all or nothing.* I went on to become part of the art community in Chicago. I had the exhibition on this side.

When in 1987 we lost Ana Mendieta, the idea of making a documentary film about her life and work filled me with strength. She was someone with whom I had felt a strong connection. Ana had also made contact with the island years before the obstacles had come down. Together with a video producer friend, I went back to film and search out the pieces that Ana had created in the Escaleras de Jaruco. It was a fascinating task that happily led us to find those sculptures. I'll never forget the afternoon when, after enduring thousands of scratches and mosquito bites as we climbed up a hill covered with brush, we found *The Black Venus* hidden behind a curtain of foliage in a small cave. At the foot of the sculpture there was a nest, and the whole floor was covered with ground snails.

The documentary was an enormous effort that carried me onto newer and newer paths. It was also a way of presenting our Cuban reality in all its complexity from the two opposing poles, from where each, to its own way of thinking, holds a piece of the story.

Pinar del Río

Far away. I fell asleep, exhausted, seated in the middle of a box next to the stage of the old provincial theater where they were staging *Santa Camila de La Habana Vieja*. There, with the play in full swing, I began to dream about the time when I was a child, spending a few days at the house of my mother's friend, Peggi, when the lights went out. Suddenly, Peggi became possessed by a saint, and she began to speak French like a Black slave. I lit a candle and followed her until we reached her bedroom. She went up to her pillow and took out a small, square object, hard like a seed. It was made of raw leather, sewn by hand. Peggi looked at me, put the object on the floor, and ordered it to jump. I was very surprised when it began to move and jump; later, when she ordered it toward me, the object, as if it were alive, shifted next to me. At that moment I felt no fear, only the certainty that there were other, invisible, powerful forces. I woke up to applause at the end of the play. I then remembered that this dream had really happened, many years before.

Santiago de Cuba

I walked in downtown Santiago, near the corner of the park by the church, amidst thousands of people, a sea of yellow, red, blue handkerchiefs. The street was on a kind of rise, and I could see the sea shining in the distance under the sun at two in the afternoon. The heat was oppressive. In the distance the *comparsa,* the Carnival team, of Los Hoyos was on its way. You could feel the drums getting closer. On their way. They were almost on top of me. They had a Chinese trumpet. Behind them the crowd rolled in. I took a photo, then another. I suddenly noticed that I was standing on a storm drain lid; written on it in relief were the words, "Santiago de Cuba, 1786." The musicians were right in front of me now, and I took the last picture before moving on. I could barely focus. My eyes were full of tears.

Someone once told me during a cleansing ceremony that, if the goat cries, they spare its life.

Sleepless

The first time I saw it was late at night, and I was surrounded by people, by friends, and by music. There was little light in the room and the only light bulb working just let you see a bit of the little painting that hung on the wall. It was a dark scene, the street that goes along the side of the University, familiar, homey, a curve and its lights. I felt what I always feel with things I like: nearby. It made me feel more like I was in Havana. Suddenly the voices around me made more sense, the references were more exact. Something had happened to me, although the night was still the same. That painting, like some small window, had glimpsed my world, my night.

The next day I waited patiently to see it again in better light. That night I had had strange dreams: of the dark sea, of the sensation of arriving, of the pervasive smell of salt; of the cold. I awoke very early, and I remember looking for my diary and writing that "this is not the golden age any more." The piece was by a Cuban painter whom I knew fairly well, thanks to the reproductions that reached my hands in Chicago. This painter knew Havana very well, could recreate it perfectly, lived in it, but had already died. It was of no particular era, although when I could place it better by the light of day, I saw it was a nocturnal scene in blues, in ochres, a bit of yellow; the street was deserted, the city asleep forever. A few days later I left Cuba.

I had a hard time situating that reality in my life on this side. When I got here, everything became chunks of a puzzle that was always missing pieces, the pieces that had stayed behind. I'd walk about the studio, remembering phrases and making up new routes, new ways of finding myself in it. I didn't see anything more by that painter, but the light from that scene and the dream of the sea remained fresh for me.

I received an invitation by way of some friends to attend the Film Festival at the end of that year. On this trip, I promised myself, I would try to investigate more deeply. I would work harder, bring home more images. I went loaded down with paper and oil crayons. I wanted and had to do some drawing for an advertising campaign for a well-known vodka company. I had no time to do it over here. I got to Havana at the beginning of December. It was 1989, and a long history in Europe was beginning, or coming to an end: Rumania would fall at the end of the year. We watched the news on the Havana TV sets: the Soviet Union was trembling. *Perestroika* and *glasnost* had their double effect on Cuba. I had a few laughs with some delightful old women in Cárdenas, who avidly listened to the news on Radio Martí. There was talk of doing a conga when the changes reached the island. We all watched change getting closer, although no one could predict that what was really approaching was the fateful Special Period. I began to feel the cold.

On this trip I had to go to see my friend who had a Víctor Manuel painting. I went back to her house and there, that afternoon, I got out the paper and started to sketch, but this time I was going to use the work as a background. Uky, my friend's son, was very enthusiastic about the idea. They now had the painting in the living room, and in the full afternoon sun it was marvelous. Right there I started working on the living room table, using the materials I had at hand: I started making my own work this way. The TV set was turned on, and the national news program was starting to broadcast a report on Moscow's monuments: The symbols of Russian communism were being broken into a thousand bits.

My drawing kept taking new directions: Two figures commanded the foreground. It was a couple coming out half-asleep into the street, the same street from the painting that so fascinated me. On their clothing I painted the moon, a fish, a bird, a wasp, a diamond, as if part of their dreams were also their clothes. In Havana the Special Period was beginning, and the few dogs in the neighborhood wouldn't stop barking.

A few days later, on the way to the airport, I saw an unforgettable sunrise. It was very early in the morning, and hundreds and hundreds of people were riding their bikes on the highway on their way to school or to work. The light was still very low and the roads full of dust. I wondered in anguish how this strange and

Illustration 5.5. Desvelada por culpa de un perro (Unable to sleep on account of a dog)

horrible era would play out for the Cubans. The airport was in chaos. People inside and out were accompanying those who were leaving. Everything went slowly. It was the familiar scene of friends, relatives, children, embracing to say goodbye, preparing for another separation. And then each was on the way to Customs and then, beyond some windows, the waiting room for boarding the next plane to Miami.

Sitting in the cafeteria behind an enormous glass window I could hear Benny Moré over the loudspeakers and the voices of the Cuban waiters asking the cook for a hamburger, a glass of orange juice. And again, the voice of Benny singing: *"...pueblo donde yo nací"* (town where I was born). Right then the plane arrived from Miami. The enormous power of the motor that brought a planeload of passengers from the other shore seemed to shake the building. Then I looked past the airplane, to the other side of the fence, and saw a crowd of people growing excited. The plane from Miami was here! The vibrations were intense.

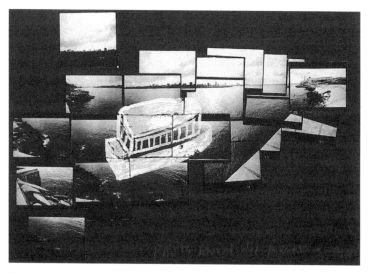

Illustration 5.6. Photo Mural del puerto (Mural of the port)

Something difficult always happens to me when I leave the island, something like when I saw my mother, fragile and nervous,
leaving me. I was going back to where I lived. I could hear a
guaracha. At a nearby table, indifferent and beautiful French women
were passing time. In the bag by my side, rolled up, a new sketch
traveled with me this time, one begun in Havana but destined to
take on a new form in Chicago.

6

From This Side of the Fish Tank

Teresa de Jesús Fernández

I BELIEVE that in the history of each of us there is a precise moment, unexpected as lightning, painful and sharp as a needle prick, in which we can, particularly situate in memory the beginning of the end of our childhood.

Passing through this long station on the road to adulthood, this last, final stop, often involves paying a terrible toll: the loss of memory, in exchange for access to maturity.[1]

I find a profound contradiction in quotation from *Trapido* cited in Maria Antoinetta Sacarino's review of *Il Bilico (Juggling)*, Barbara Trapido's book on adolescence, which has always reminded me of my favorite novels, *Le grand Meaulnes* and *Catcher in the Rye*. If anything is *not* lost during this difficult transit to adolescence, it is memory. For just this reason, reading this review made me remember when I was sixteen, in the last days of March 1978, and the departure of Gigi, María, and Carlitos was imminent. We grew up together, two parallel families; our parents were very close friends, and from the time we were small, we were used to spending every weekend in one of our two houses.

I preferred theirs, at 31st and 34th, so different from mine: just as large but more modern and with a super mirror in Berta's room that covered the whole wall. I'd generally throw myself down on Berta's bed to watch Gigi and my older sister getting dressed to go to a party to which María and I would never go because we were too small, but at the time we didn't care one bit because we had a great gang: the Montoto twins, Maruchi, Juanita, Betty, and her cousin.

Early each Sunday morning we'd bike to The Loma de los Paticos near the Almendares River, then head downhill at top speed, resisting the temptation to use the brakes; or, some afternoons, we'd make prank phone calls or ring the doorbell at the Martínez house and rush off in every possible direction. This made us feel daring and very happy.

We became adolescents, and our dates moved to Saturday nights, to the endless peregrination from party to party, to slow dances with the lights turned down and the songs of José Feliciano and Roberto Carlos, as strictly forbidden for us as the songs of the Beatles had been for the generation before ours. With adolescence also came our first uncertainties and stronger convictions.

One day I came home, and they were talking about "the departure." In Cuba, for many years and even today, "the departure" has meant someone is leaving the country for good; I knew of a few families who were waiting to leave, but they were never people I considered important or essential to my life. Leaving meant giving up. Those who left had to give up their work, their house, all the things they had that weren't strictly personal and necessary, their relatives who stayed behind, their country. When I found out that this time they were talking about "the departure" of Berta and her family, my world came crashing down. They were telling me that at some still-undefined moment I was to lose my childhood companions, our weekends on 34th Street, our long conversations on the front porch on 20th Street, the parties, the secrets—in two words, our friendship.

Some of my most wrenching memories belong to this stage in my life: the last night we slept under the same roof, this time at my house; the group of friends going to the airport; the hugs, the last words we said to each other and could not hear because we were separated by an enormous window, glacial, marginalizing, and alienating us. It was humanly impossible for me to stop loving them or thinking of them because of a simple choice of staying or leaving.

All I could do was observe the vacuum they had left, observe how hard it was to pass in front of their house every day on the way to high school and see it unceremoniously occupied by strangers, or to know that the number 29-1919 was crossed out in my family's phone book. This was the beginning of an endless incision. It was also the first time I was aware of what it meant to see people you love go abroad and how absurd it was that they were leaving forever.

Exile is usually understood as being uprooted; viewed this way, only those who leave suffer, those who voluntarily or involuntarily give up their native soil. It is the condition of all who emigrate, who live apart from their own nations; but this is an incomplete definition. It does not take into account the other side of the phenomenon, that of the Other, the internal exile, who is left with the estrangement, the sense of loss; it is the Other who is left to deal with absence.

One afternoon almost a year later I went to the Ambassador cinema with some friends. I don't remember the name of the feature film, but I have never forgotten the documentary they showed with it: "55 Hermanos," directed by Jesús Díaz. It was about a group of young Cuban-Americans returning from the United States to their country for the first time after many years. Most had left as young children with their parents, others had been sent alone during Operation Pedro Pan, and now they were back in Cuba, filled with expectations, talking about their experiences, how their reconciliation with their home country had come about, the rupture with their parents, and how difficult it had been for them.

I remember my astonishment: I was a member of the Young Communists Union (Unión de Jóvenes Comunistas), and the return of those young people indicated, in some way, the tiniest opening that went beyond dogmas and preconceptions.

The documentary was a bit forced, not sufficiently spontaneous, reconciliatory but polemical and rhetorical. At its best moments, however, it was quite moving, because there they were with their personal histories, their uncontained emotions, amazed at their memories, surprised at rediscovering the places of their childhoods and finding that the real dimensions were different from what they remembered, that everything was the same, yet different, and above all, "a lot tinier."

This was my second contact with exile reality, but this time it was more: It was a concept, because they conceptualized it, spoke of what they had lived through in terms of conflicts, issues, consciousness, politicization. It was another reading of the problem.

There they were, present at that moment by the art of film, and I felt a mixture of empathy and rage because I could understand them, perceive the loneliness they had suffered, the disquiet, the displacement, the nostalgia, the sadness, the helplessness. All this brought us close together, yet we were watching them in that false cinematic presence when in reality they were already back in those other cities so many miles away, living in that space that was hostile to them but that they had somehow already tamed, while my friends and I were seated here in this Havana cinema, grieving for them and for ourselves.

It is hard to explain because of the complexity of the situation. That documentary was telling me that perhaps on some future day I would again see the people who had left, and this thought filled me with hope for a change for the better, but I was strangely bothered that those young people should talk of Nation and Revolution and grand ideals and even allow themselves a few critical remarks (which we young people on the inside could not have made without being frowned upon) from the comfort of exile. Nation and revolution and ideals had to be lived in order to understand how much they were costing us, and I had the feeling that this particular detail hadn't been taken into account.

I don't know to what degree my rage at that moment was justified; in truth, what mattered most to me was trying to figure out

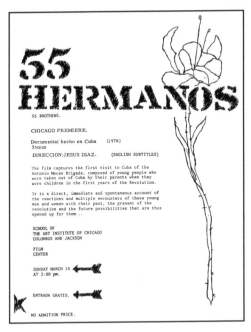

Illustration 6.1. Leaflet for the film 55 Hermanos

its significance of *"55 Hermanos,"* which at the national level translated into the positive existence of the Cuban community abroad, the metamorphosis of *"gusanos"* into "butterflies," the slogan *La Patria ha crecido* (The Nation has grown), and the first ideological/emotional upheaval of the Cubans on the island.

It is curious how quickly some projects mature and wither. The Dialog that opened in 1977 between a group of young Cuban-Americans and the government of Cuba emerged from humanity and intelligence (although to think there were no other interests at work would be naive), from democracy and tolerance, from political clarity. Recognizing and legitimizing the Cuban community abroad (the euphemistic term), without pigeonholing them all as unpatriotic, demonstrated a move toward understanding, but it gradually turned into a matter of economic interest, whether in the bosom of the families who initiated the distinction between those who had relatives in "the community" abroad and those who did not; or in the hard-cash (dollar) stores (some for the community, others for diplomats and other foreigners); or in the escalating cost of airplane tickets and hotel rooms in Cuba.

Throughout 1979 many Cubans came to the island from the United States, and for the Cubans on the island it was a shock to see all these people loaded down with huge suitcases, with photos to show how well they had all done, and hundreds of dollars to spend on gifts. Somehow this reality, though it was in some cases false, belied the prevailing vision of the position of the Cuban exiles; up to that moment it was generally believed that even if some were doing well, above all the upper-class families who had emigrated at the beginning of the Revolution, the majority had to work hard to survive in a life filled with insecurity and fear. Finding out that many of the people coming back had left Cuba with nothing but their own ability to work created a different opinion (no less false than the former, for so many reasons that I won't bother to specify them) of what exile had to offer, and this new conception and valorization of the lives of Cuban exiles gave rise to the inevitable comparison between the apparent or actual standard of living in the United States, and the difficult reality of daily life within Cuba.

I am convinced that among the multiple causes of the exodus of 1980, two were the most explosive: One was the conflict born in the consciousness of Cubans who, after repudiating their own relatives as traitors, saw them return "triumphant" and bearing so many "goods"; the other was the repressive campaign—so reminiscent of the sadly famous Grey Period—which we young students in Cuba all knew as the Process of Deepening Communist Consciousness.

At the end of 1979 I was 19 years old and a second-year student majoring in education with specializations in Spanish and Literature. In December the Union de Jouenes Comunistas (UJC; Union of Young Communists) of the University Pedagogical Institute held its Evaluation Assembly, and I was invited to attend by the

First Secretary of the National UJC at the time, Luis Orlando Domínguez. It was then that we were informed of the purification campaign that would be carried out among the membership and later extended to all the young students in the country, through assemblies that would take place in every middle school, high school, and university.

The Process of Deepening Communist Consciousness was created to eradicate, first, from the ranks of the Young Communists Union and then from the schools, especially the universities, every student who was considered a *persona non grata,* a negative element, a non-revolutionary. The promoter of this campaign against corruption and ideological deviation was Luis Orlando Domínguez,[2] and I remember the hard-line speech in which he accused the youth in general of having lost the spirit of self-criticism and of combativeness, and accused us of having let ourselves be seduced by the false values of consumerism and capitalism.

Putting the Process into practice had dreadful consequences; many of us lost our membership in the UJC, and others were expelled from the universities under the most baseless pretexts and for the most preposterous of reasons. This was due to the mediocrity of many of the leaders and other members, to political opportunism—an evil that has always plagued us—and revanchist injustice.

What most shook me at that moment was the prevailing lack of coherence in the assemblies; in the most extremist of them, they went so far as to take unconstitutional measures, for even though the Constitution of the Republic of Cuba prohibits racial and sexual discrimination and establishes freedom of religion, between December 1979 and March 1980, students were expelled for suspicion of homosexuality or for being practicing Catholics.

The next few years after this experience and the Mariel exodus, I watched almost all my friends from childhood and adolescence leave. The group living abroad grew greater and greater. I often fantasized about the possibility of getting together again in the front hall of my house, as we used to do more than fifteen years ago, talking all night long until daybreak about what had happened during their long absence. Somewhere in my house there is a photo that shows almost all of us piled up in one corner of the hall. The only ones still here in Cuba are Lin, Sergito, my brother, my sisters, and I. Sometimes I think that exile reality, at least so far as my emotional world is concerned, grew up with me from that faraway year of 1978, and was consolidated years later in 1983,[3] when I met a group of Cuban-Americans in the Antonio Maceo Brigade.

An intense poem by Lourdes Casal contains these verses:

> But New York wasn't the city of my childhood.
> I carry this marginality, immune to all turning back,
> too *habanera* to be *newyorkina*,
> too *newyorkina* to be
> —even to become again—
> anything else.

I believe that for those who have only experienced exile from the position of never having crossed the fish tank but having watched everyone else cross, these verses are disquieting. For those who have lived the exile experience themselves, they reflect its very drama. It is like living in suspense, in that dual space where reminiscences of what went on in your place of origin—a kind of unconditioned reflex—flow together with newly acquired references that with the passage of time become equally solid, yet never solid enough to absorb and erase the past. You can never give it up for good; nothing is more tenacious than memory. That is what Lourdes Casal's words reveal: "too much from Havana . . . too much a New Yorker.

Meeting a few people who had left Cuba as small children made me see this other side of exile. What surprised me in them was how jealously they conserved in their memories details that seemed insignificant to me, or how precisely they remembered some area of the city, the names of the streets, a piece of music, a tree, a smell. I discovered that they had a different way of looking at things; more than just seeing them, they imprinted them, stored them away. At first their behavior disconcerted me; later, I was frightened to think that if I should some day find myself in the same situation, I would not have all those sharply focused images. I started being more careful about how I experienced my own city.

For ten years now I have lived and worked outside of Cuba, returning during vacations. There are days when the distance seems unbearable, and others when I can identify with the city I am living in and I realize that there, too, I have my own space.

I sometimes become lost in thought about what I call my parallel lives, but I always think that for me this experience is strictly demarcated in time, that I can always return to terra firma. This conviction sustains me and makes me feel privileged, even though there is a place in my memory that I maintain intact and full of heartsickness—that place of "the beginning of the end of our childhood—for the friends who left; for those I met after they returned to Cuba, I keep this other dimension of memories and nostalgia.

Notes

1. From Maria Antonietta Sacarino, "La Talpalibri" (Supplement) (Il Manifesto, Thursday, November 16, 1995). A review of *In bilico,* the Italian translation of *Juggling,* the fourth novel by South African novelist Barbara Trapido.

2. The Cuban critic and essayist Ambrosio Fornet coined the term *Período Gris,* "Grey Period," to refer to the time from 1968 (officially titled the Year of the Revolutionary Offensive) to 1971, when the Congress on Education and Culture took place. From the economic point of view, it was during the Revolutionary Offensive that it was decided to eliminate free and private enterprise and to nationalize or close down small businesses, considered the deadweight of capitalist society. From that moment the State became the sole producer and distributor of consumer goods and services. In the ideological arena and the intellectual and art worlds, those were particularly dark years, marked by the repression of homosexuals and of anyone considered outside "Communist morality" (long hair on men, listening to the Beatles, and other ab-

surdities were considered socially negative acts). This was the time of the Padilla case involving the Cuban poet, writer, and translator Herberto Padilla, who has lived in exile since 1980, and of the isolation of other Cuban intellectuals who lived for more than a decade segregated inside their own country without being able to publish their works—Antón Arrufat, Pablo Armando Fernández, César López, among others.

3. Presently serving a 20-year prison sentence for embezzlement of government funds.

4. In that year I was a third-year philology student in the Faculty of Arts and Letters of the University of Havana. I had switched to that faculty in 1980 after being expelled from the UJC in the Pedagogical Institute for "affection," a pretty shabby way of not accusing me directly of homosexuality. In May of 1983 a group of Cuban Americans were in Cuba, among them some of the founders of the journal Areíto, to celebrate the tenth anniversary of its founding, and I had the opportunity to meet them in my house. At that time I began a deep and long friendship with some of them, in particular, Sonia Rivera and Nereida García Ferraz. After that first meeting and many times later I would meet Nena Torres, Mariana Gastón, and so many others.

7

Through Other Looking Glasses
Josefina de Diego

> *Exile is living in a place where there is no house in which we were ever children.*
>
> —LOURDES CASAL, *PALABRAS JUNTAN REVOLUCIÓN*

The Story of My Abuela Berta

I'VE BEEN used to hearing the English language since I was born. My paternal grandmother Berta and her four brothers emigrated as young children to the United States at the close of the nineteenth century because of the war with Spain, and they lived in New York for more than ten years. When Abuela returned to Cuba she barely remembered her Spanish. Her childhood songs were all in English, as were the names of the games she played, her prayers; she thought in English. She never adapted. She missed the libraries, the customs, the food, the snow, Santa Claus, and Christmas. When she was twenty she married an Austrian in Havana, and they combined their nostalgias.

Abuela died at the age of ninety. The night before she fell into a coma, she told me one more time, with enviable lucidity, of that afternoon in New York when she first saw "a carriage that drove without horses." She taught English to her son, my father, because she couldn't imagine being in his company without that odd underground river of communication that can only be established through the nuances of one's first language. When she wrote him letters she addressed them, "Dearest Son." She combined the two languages into a jargon that became very dear to us. She was a tireless reader, but she only read novels in English. Her favorites were those of Charles Dickens and Lewis Carroll. When Papá would knock on the door of her room, you could hear her happy voice saying, "No room! No room!" To which Papá immediately would reply, "'There's plenty of room,' cried Alice indignantly!" But she was not satisfied with just knowing the language. She studied and taught it and eventually came to be Inspector General of English for the country. She also wished to teach it to us, her three grandchildren. Our little neighborhood friends made fun of us because she talked to us in an incomprehensible tongue. English became an everyday, family matter.

Many years later, in 1978, I reencountered that "jargon" among the young members of the Antonio Maceo Brigade. Abuela died three years later, in August 1981, but perhaps there is a little of my grandmother Berta in the way each one of them speaks.

First Goodbyes—Our Departure

My parents were teachers. My grandmother Berta had published an English textbook in three volumes, *Exercises in Functional Grammar,* which guaranteed a fair income. It was not a life of luxury, but we didn't lack anything. The house was like an amusement park.

In January 1959, my family went through the same things as other families who were not necessarily upper class. After the end of the Second World War and the beginning of the Cold War, anticommunist propaganda was on the upswing. You were always hearing about patria *potestad* and the terrible things the communists did. In the newspaper *Revolución,* Saturday, July 18, 1959, Fidel Castro emphatically denied the accusations against him and affirmed that "our Revolution isn't red but olive green, the color of the uniform of the Rebel Army." There were strong suspicions to the contrary, however. The private schools were closed, so we had no religious education. Catholicism was associated with the bourgeoisie, religiousness with ideological weakness. My parents were Catholics and decided to leave the country.

The first to leave were my grandmother Berta's nephews and nieces, whom she loved deeply. Friends, neighbors, and acquaintances left, too. At the age of ten I said a tearful goodbye, without understanding very well just why, to my two best friends, Lucía and Miriam. I have never heard from them again. I still feel ill when I go to the airport, even if it is to pick up someone very dear. It brings me bad memories. As my brother, Lichi, says, leaving Cuba was not a *destierro* but an *entierro,* not a banishment but a burial. It tore you apart completely. You didn't just abandon the country, the house you had always lived in, your best memories, secret hideouts, photos, books, toys. You abandoned your family with the certainty that you would never see them again. And that is just what happened in most cases. My uncle Agustin never again saw his mother or his brothers, and he is tormented by the knowledge that they lived another thirty years without him and he without them. It was not until many years later that they could begin to dream about returning. (I remember that on the application to study at the university, among such questions as name, address, and sex, were two, included toward the end like a poorly sewn-on patch, that would determine—and we all knew this—the acceptance decision: 1. Do you have relatives in the United States and do you maintain contact with them? And 2. do you have a religious affiliation? To maintain contact with your relatives was in the least a delicate matter.) But not everyone speaks of this reality. They prefer to say with some contempt, "Why did they leave? Nobody forced them to." This way they ease their consciences. Leaving has never been, nor is it now, an easy decision for anyone.

I will never forget the tension in my house, the conversations held in whispers so the children wouldn't hear the quiet sobbing of my grandmother Josefina, my mother's fathomless sorrow. The decision was made. My parents, my brothers, my grandmother Berta, and I would leave for the United States. My uncles,

Illustration 7.1. Salud Publica (Public Health) document

my maternal grandmother, and my cousins would stay behind. I didn't really understand then—later I found out—why the house had to be stripped bare, and why it had to be done secretly, as if it were a crime. The word "inventory" was constantly mentioned, and everything that had to be done before the famous inventory. Like thieves in the night, my parents loaded the car with the few valuable possessions we had—the television, the porch curtains, paintings, books, some furniture—and took them to the homes of friends and relatives. At any moment the inspector could show up and coldly take note of all he would see in the house, and he would seal the front door to show that the inventory has been done. Once the exit permits arrived, the inventory was repeated, and if anything was missing, they would cancel the exit permits. I remember the way he looked at us, with distance, as if he were dealing with delinquents, as if he had the right to invade our privacy or intimacy. My parents had to resign their jobs, and then we had to wait for the telegram with the notification of our departure date. It was to be June 4, 1962, and we would fly out on KLM airlines. The winter clothes were bought and the suitcases packed. The house seemed a dance hall, but without music, without joy.

The only one who was happy was my grandmother Berta, for whom leaving meant regaining what the rest of us would lose: her memories, her roots.

In the end, the trip did not happen. My mother would have gone with us, but she was leaving behind the rest of her family, and her health was not holding up. A diabetic for many years, her attacks of hyperglycemia multiplied, and her blood sugar levels spun out of control. The doctor who attended her told my father that if we left we would save ourselves from communism but run the risk of being motherless. The suitcases were unpacked, and the house fixed up again. My grandmother Berta at last renounced her past and, between tears and laughter, uncorked the bottle of French champagne she had set aside for our departure.

Even though we had renounced the idea of leaving the country, which was always considered a kind of treason, the "original sin" of having once attempted to leave, dogged us for many years. It was a "sin" that could never be pardoned, not even for us who were just children and bore no responsibility at all. In 1973, during a meeting with my fellow students at the University of Havana, I had to make a public explanation of the causes that had led my parents to make that decision. Just as in a confessional with a priest, but instead surrounded by many witnesses, I had to make excuses for my parents and make it very clear that they had made a mistake and that they were now "integrated" (a very fashionable word at the time) perfectly to the revolutionary process. "Absolution" never arrived. In 1978 I was nominated to head a department in a cultural institution. A few days before being confirmed, I received an odd official notice. I was to appear in an important government office at five in the afternoon. When I entered, a nasty-looking functionary tossed a file on her desk that opened, as if by magic, to a page on which I saw myself at the age of ten. It was a photocopy of the solicitation form for Definitive Departure from the Country, which my parents had presented sixteen years before. The photograph was the one that appears in my passport, which I still keep. The functionary asked me:

"Do you have any knowledge of this?"

"Yes. Why?"

"No reason," she answered, a bit perturbed. "It's just that many people are surprised, because they assure us that they didn't know anything about that situation."

"And . . . ?" I began to ask her.

"You may leave, *compañera*," she ordered me, dryly.

I never understood what they meant to do with this "information."

Paradoxically, it was at that same time that a turning point came in relations with the Cuban community abroad, with the future "butterflies." In December of the previous year, the Antonio Maceo Brigade had made their first visit to the island. The sin was not the same, or perhaps it was the sentence that made things different.

"Curiouser and curiouser," I thought, remembering my grandmother and her quotations from the restless Alice.

Meeting the Young People of the Antonio Maceo Brigade (Some Anecdotes)

Relations between the government and those who "left" (or those who are leaving) have always been tense and hostile. For many years, from 1959 to 1978 (and, I suspect, even today in certain strategic sectors), there was a prohibition against communicating with your family in the United States either by letter or phone. Not that they sent you to jail: My grandmother kept in touch with her family, just like many other Cubans, up until her death; but maintaining that kind of relationship with the "disaffected" automatically made you a *persona no confiable,* an untrustworthy person. That kind of classification could keep you from being employed in certain areas, moving up the ladder in your own job, entering the university, joining the Party ranks or the Young Communists Union, or traveling abroad (which could be done only on professional business or by personal invitation after you reached the age of 60 or 65, depending on your sex). Relations

with foreigners were also frowned upon, as if the diseases of capitalism were contagious, like a cold or the plague.

For various reasons, these hatreds and fears were not felt in my
house. My father, a writer well known both inside Cuba and beyond, was constantly visited by intellectuals from every corner of
the globe, from the "Soviéticos," as we used to call them, to the
"Americanos," as they have always been called. My brothers and I
worked in cultural institutions, which were more liberal and tolerant, bur I think that we were influenced above all by the "open-
door" style that we inherited from my mother's side of the family and into which my father and his mother assimilated perfectly.
Grandmother Josefina, a graduate of the Orbón Conservatory,
was a great pianist. Opera singers of Cuban and Spanish music
were always hanging around the house, asking her to stage their
repertoire. Her house was also frequented by painters, writers,
and my mother's and uncle's university friends. My *abuelita* was,
despite the conventions of the time, fairly liberal. Her habit was
to trust first and to distrust hardly ever. There was always some
homeless relative or friend to take in, and so her house was known
as the "Hotel Badía," after her last name. I think that all these circumstances were what made my house a very special place for the
young people returning to their country after many years.

In 1975, I met Lourdes Casal, a writer and the author of *Palabras Juntan Revolución*.[1] She was also the founder of *Areíto* magazine. Lourdes succeeded through her intelligence, lucidity and
personal charm to get close to us and bring others to Cuba. She
heard about us from a mutual North American friend and thus began winding the intricate ball of yarn that led my family, my
friends, and I to establish contact in the summer of 1978 with
members of the Antonio Maceo Brigade. I met Vivian first and
then all the rest.

My grandmother Berta loved to talk with them in English, and
she would ask them the most incredible things. Her favorite question was whether "elevated railroads" still existed. The New York
of her childhood had changed, but some spaces had almost hero-

ically survived the passage of time. Nothing made her happier than to know that some of her favorite places still existed. My brothers and I were startled to think that our life stories might have been the same as those of the *brigadistas*.

My house was turned into a kind of "emergency quarters." Located in the middle of El Vedado, it became an important meeting point. I remember one time when about twenty of them showed up. My mother, used to giving shelter to any friend of ours, called me, with great mystery, into my room. I was worried because I thought something had upset her.

"What is it?" I asked.

"There's lots of them, *mi'jita*," she said.

"Lots?"

"Yes, and I don t have enough sheets or towels. What are we going to do?"

"Don t worry," I said, relieved. "Just three or four of them are going to stay."

Another day I arrived from work at six in the afternoon, tired and sweaty. I was about to go into my room when I heard my father's voice, panting as he ran down the hallway.

"Don t go in!" he almost shouted.

"Why not?" I asked, a bit upset. "What is it?"

"Silvia is sleeping in there," he replied.

"Silvia? I don t know anyone named Silvia," I answered, half-irritated and half-intrigued.

"Neither do we. She doesn't know you, either. But she said she's a friend of V., from the Brigade, and she was exhausted. We felt sorry for her, so we let her come in."

Silvia, who was obviously worn out, slept in my room until nine that night.

Most of the young people who returned to Cuba with the brigades spoke perfect Spanish, but a few had serious problems in making themselves understood. Tomas didn't speak a word. He had memories of the country and of his school, but his parents had taken him away as a small child; his language was English. I saw him only once. He asked me to take him to his old place in the Siboney development and handed me a piece of paper with the address. The house, on the outskirts of Miramar, was small-ish, with peeling paint, broken windows, and a generally de-plorable aspect. Tomas did not recognize it.

"This isn't my house," he declared emphatically, in English.

"But this is the right address," I argued, paper in hand.

"Can't be. There must be some mistake."

We went up and down the neighborhood, street by street. Tomas looked over all the houses trying to discover the house of his childhood games. After wandering for more than an hour, he asked me to take him back to the first address, where the dilapi-dated building stood.

"Please, just leave me here, and don't wait," he begged, with reddened eyes. He sat down on the curb in front of the house and stayed there, more disconcerted than sad, in a silent and heartrending dialog with his former home.

Sarah had one obsession: to return to live in Cuba. She had made up her mind, but first she had to spend a long time in her aunt and uncle's house, living like any other Cuban. She wanted to test herself, to see if she could do it, and so she made it a prin-ciple never to buy anything in the dollar stores. When I went to visit, she offered me Coronilla, cheap rum that you could buy *por la libre* on the open market; or "mixed" coffee; or a delicious pea soup, for Sarah was an excellent cook. On one occasion I arrived at her house when she had just taken a shower. "You smell of Fi-esta shampoo," I told her, speaking of a brand that was sold only in the stores for Cubans. She took my comment as the highest praise.

For me, the idea was totally illogical, and not for political rea-sons or because of the shortage of goods, but because of some-thing much deeper: Sarah, like my grandmother Berta, had her roots in New York. Her habits and customs were familiar to me, and every day I found something new in her. Sarah's friends in the United States were Dutch, Koreans, Italians. She was an expert at

Asian cooking and was always inviting me to eat delicious dishes from those countries, which she made with the vegetables she found in the markets. "Ah, Chinese food!" I'd comment, displaying my utter ignorance of these details. "No, Japanese!" Sarah would groan. She was one of the first to get around all over town on her bike, something that at the time seemed completely outdated. Truly passionate about the world of news—just like my grandmother—she was capable of waking up at dawn just to listen to European stations that began broadcasting at that early hour.

I never found out why she wasn't able to get permission to stay, despite her desiring it so much and for so long. I don't know whether she herself might have rejected it. The last time we spoke, some years ago, she mentioned that she was thinking of moving.

"Where to?" I asked.

"Nepal," she said.

"What do you mean, Nepal?" I asked, confused.

Quickly, guessing my fears, she replied: "Don't worry, I already checked it all out. Letters take as long to reach Nepal as they do from Havana: one month!"

Fortunately, she did not move to Nepal but to a remote state in the northwest United States. She was farther away than ever from Cuba—farther away, but not more distant.

In 1982 my father was invited by the New York Center for Cuban Studies and the Círculo de Cultura Cubana to give a series of lectures on literature at various North American universities. Many of the *brigadistas* were professors at those universities and formed part of the organizing committee. The trip was planned like a grand conspiracy, because they were trying to kill several birds with one stone: to bring my father to the United States, a country he had not visited since his honeymoon in 1948 and where he had friends and relatives whom he had not seen for more than twenty years; to introduce him as a poet to an audience that did not know him; and, above all, to give themselves the pleasure of inviting him to their homes. For all these young people loved him dearly. My father was, I sincerely believe, a great writer, but he was also a very simple man, not conceited, or, at most, vain in an innocent, almost childlike way. He listened to everyone with equal affection and respect. That is how he received the members of Antonio Maceo Brigade. His trip to the United States was charged with powerful and sad emotions that might have affected his health had it not been for the company and care of these youths. "Your friends are always by my side, and it's as if I am finding you everywhere," he wrote me from Chicago. And they stayed by his side, right up to the day of his death.

Lourdes Casal

"I'm full of plans," she assured us with a smile just weeks before she died. And it was true. Her yearning to work and her indomitable cheerfulness kept life from "scattering away" from her, as she said, sooner than the doctors had predicted. That afternoon she had asked us, my father and me, to take her to the Book Fair that was being held in La Habana Vieja around the bookstore La Moderna Poesía. Lourdes made the most of this outing, bought some books in an auction, walked with her cane around every nook of the Fair. We left her back at the hospital late at night. Her kidneys had not functioned for years, and she needed dialysis treatments that left her very weak. It was then that she asked me to help her. Her relapses were becoming more frequent.

The young people from the Brigade were always visiting her, as were her friends from Havana and the United States. She never lacked for company. We were all interested, very interested, in her opinions. I remember that I went to see her at the Clinical Surgery Hospital at 26th and Boyeros after the events at the Peruvian Embassy in the midst of "acts of repudiation" on the streets. I was very worried. Lourdes was, too. Talking with her calmed me down and soothed me. That was her gift. I was also interested in her views on poetry and literature in general, and from time to time I would ask her advice about my private life.

*Illustration 7.2. Lourdes Casal (sitting down) with
Josefina de Diego (standing to the left), 1980*

Lourdes, whose hours, as she well knew, were numbered, listened to everyone and always set aside time for others, but her illness was advancing, and she was becoming weaker every day. I knew English, thanks to my grandmother Berta's lessons, so I wrote letters for her. Her health had deteriorated to the point that she could not hold a pen in her hands. Nor could she tape her own voice, because she didn't have the strength to press the buttons on the machine. And she absolutely had to finish that book on terrorism she had proposed to publish after the assassination of Carlos Muñiz Varela, the boy with "the intense, intelligent gaze" as she described him in one of her poems. Carlos, a member of the

Antonio Maceo Brigade and director of a travel agency in Puerto Rico, was shot down after leaving his house in April 1979, by people sickened with hatred who did not want the trips to Cuba. She was never able to finish her book. I wrote her last letters three days before her death. She was telling a North American friend about the happy time she had had at the New Year's celebrations, and she asked for some important facts on various terrorist acts that had taken place in the United States.

Those of us who knew her will never get used to her silence, and we will miss, always, the warm clarity of her smile.

Stop and Go, or, The Influence of the Tides

At the end of 1978 and throughout 1979 the buried dream of many Cubans was revived: It was now possible to return to the island. Thousands of families that had been divided for more than twenty years got together again. Grandchildren met grandparents; memories became realities. My house continued to be the "emergency quarters," the "Hotel Diego" of the young *brigadistas*.

Then, something unexpected happened in May of 1980. Certain desperate, irresponsible persons burst into the Peruvian Embassy, riddling one of its guards with bullets. At that point, one of the saddest and most violent chapters in our history began. The government decided to remove its protection from the embassy, allowing thousands of Cubans to freely enter the compound. It is calculated that one person entered every fifteen seconds. In a matter of hours the Peruvian grounds had been seized, and not merely by "lumpens, antisocials, and homosexuals," as a lamentable editorial in the newspaper *Granma Internacional* (April 6, 1980) declared. As they entered they would heave back over the wall their Party cards and Young Communists Union IDs. It was an utter and unstoppable stampede. The "acts of repudiation" organized by the government only served to create more dissidents and more non-believers. People mobilized by official organizations closed down the homes of those who had decided to leave.

They put offensive graffiti on their walls, not just political sayings; they cut their electricity, water, and gas; and they threw eggs at them and beat them up. The Mariel exodus, like a swollen sea, swept away more than 125,000 Cubans to the shores of Miami in less than three months. The good-byes had begun again.

All of this was blamed, unjustly, on the blossoming "butterflies" who had returned to the island with bulging suitcases and wallets, creating an image of comfort and prosperity that did not correspond in every case to reality. The Cuban exiles in the United States had always counted on privileges that put them in an advantageous position relative to other Latin American exiles. (Remember the Cuban Adjustment Act of 1966.) But on the island a deep-set illness had been building up over many years, and it exploded in combination with the return of "the community."

The failure of the Ten-Million-Ton Sugar Harvest of 1970 brought about a national state of frustration. In 1972 Cuba joined the Council for Mutual Economic Assistance (COMECON), an association of the so-called socialist bloc. This alignment brought some important financial benefits, but its cost was an underlying servility to those other countries that many found disgusting. To be fair, however, it also put us in contact with their cultures; many good friends remain as a legacy of this alignment. The problems of corruption that were detected in the 1960s became more acute. In 1979, the Minister of Armed Forces, Raúl Castro, delivered a strongly worded speech in which he denounced this situation, and shortly afterwards more than ten ministers were removed from office. The purge began with the Minister of Public Health and the Minister of Transportation.

The escape valve that was opened at Mariel proved too powerful. The violence in the streets was frightening. The government called a meeting of "revolutionary reaffirmation" in the Plaza of the Revolution, attended by bureaucrats, foreign guests, and the "general public." Curiously, one of the angriest and most eloquent allegations was delivered by the First Secretary of the Young Communists Union at the time, Luis Orlando Domínguez.

In his speech he said, more or less, "It doesn't matter! Let them go! Sooner or later their kids will return as new members of the Antonio Maceo Brigade!" Yet the one who seemed to be planning to leave and never return was Luis Orlando himself, who, seven years later, was sentenced to twenty years in prison for a series of fraud and corruption charges. These accusations—and the report of the scandalous flight of General Rafael del Pino, hero of Playa Girón, with his entire family in a Cuban Air Force plane—were made by Fidel Castro himself before the television cameras.

In May 1985, Radio Martí began broadcasting. Cuba reacted energetically with a series of measures, including suspending the flights to the island for the Cuban community abroad. Also lumped into this "bag" of defensive measures were the young people of the Antonio Maceo Brigade, who for eight years had been trying to show that exiles were not a "monolithic bloc." Now, once more, they were not allowed to return to their country. Fortunately, this prohibition did not last long, nor was it long before some of those who had left in the Mariel flotilla returned for visits.

The 1980s, a sinister decade that will no doubt be remembered as the decade of disillusionment, brought no relief. In 1983, the United States invaded Grenada, a small Caribbean island more or less the size of one of the Florida Keys. As a result of the invasion, twenty-four Cuban engineers working there were killed. Cuba's "most glorious armed forces," as they were known, suffered a humiliating defeat. The soldiers, headed by Colonel Tortoló, who had been sent to protect the workers, ran away and sought refuge in the Soviet Embassy instead of organizing the resistance. The *Comandante* (Fidel) wanted a heroic confrontation by the construction workers, but they disobeyed his slogan of fatherland or death and instead chose life over death in a war that was not theirs.

In 1985, word of *perestroika* and *glasnost* began to arrive. The absolute governmental control of the media had made it impossible to hear other than "official" versions of what was happening around the world. For twenty-five years, Cubans had been convinced that the Soviet Union and the other socialist countries were real paradises. When *Novedades de Moscú,* a newspaper we used to buy to wrap our trash, started publishing all the horrors of Stalinism and post-Stalinism, the newspaper started selling like hot buns. To stop the poison from intoxicating the minds of the surprised readers, the government suspended the importation of all Soviet publications. In May 1989, Chinese tanks swept away the students of Tianamen Square. The images went all over the world, but they never got to Cuba. On July 13, the former General of the Revolutionary Armed Forces, Arnaldo Ochoa, and three other officials were executed by firing squad for committing "hostile acts against the state." The death penalty had been decided before the trial.

On December 7 of the same year came the burial ceremony commemorating 2,200 Cubans who had fallen in the wars in Africa. In those same days, the "socialist bloc" fell. The world contemplated, open-mouthed, the fall of the Berlin Wall and the settling of accounts with Ceaucescu and his wife during the coldest and bloodiest Christmas season ever in Rumania. The tide of disasters continued in the 1990s, with the break-up of the Soviet Union. Cuba's economic situation turned critical. The Special Period Times of Peace was declared at the end of 1990, which meant greater austerity in food, energy, and gasoline consumption. In summer of 1994, because of a drastic reduction in the standard of living and the same constant bombardment by North American radio propaganda, the *"balsero* crisis" was set in motion. On improvised rafts made of pieces of wood, tied with whatever, they set sail, as if going to a party. Some would get stuck, and the waves would simply wash them ashore. Others were not so lucky, and only parts of their rafts would return.

All these events were *lived* by the brigadistas and former brigadistas. Nobody had to talk about them. From one visit to the next they were "sowing" their own history. These were no longer the diffuse memories of childhood. The country was perfectly hinged to their lives. Alongside the political events, which of course each of them interpreted in his or her own way, other things were happening—everyday, normal things. They celebrated the new year, birthdays,

KLM

ROYAL DUTCH AIRLINES

EMPRESAS AEREAS, S. A.
AGENTES

TEL. 8-5570 · CABLE TRANSAERA
RESERVACIONES: 8-3142

TROCADERO NO. 55
HAVANA, CUBA

A las Autoridades del Aeropuerto
"José Martí"
Rancho Boyeros. Habana

S e ñ o r e s :

Hemos sido notificados por nuestra Oficina de ....MIAMI....................

que el (los) pasajero (s) ...MARIA JOSEFINA DE DIEGO Y GARCIA MARRUZ....

ha (n) sido autorizado (s) a viajar a ....MIAMI................

sin el requisito del cuño de la visa en el pasaporte por las autorida-

des de ese país.

Lo cual hacemos constar a los efectos pertinentes.

Frank Fin

Firma del Funcion...
que certifica.

K.L.M.
DUTCH AIRLINES
AGENT 37776
Empresas Aereas S.A.
HAVANA

La Habana ....13.... de ...Noviembre.... de ...1961....

Illustration 7.3. KLM travel document

carnivals; they watched dawn arrive from the *el malecón* seawall; they had "close encounters" of all kinds; they worked, did research in libraries, visited museums, attended film and theater and music festivals, slept in their homes. There were other tales to tell, happy and sad, of today and of a very recent yesterday. Never again would anyone seize from them their parents' land or their own land.

For me, meeting some of these young people meant recovering very dear friends, friends who, as my father would say, "enlarge time for us." The "chance concurrence"[2] that once took them away now brought them back, in a magical ebbing of the tide, to remain among us always.

I have often wondered what my life would have been like had we boarded the KLM flight on that fourth of June 1962. What would have become of my brothers, my parents, my grandmother? Through my friendships with the young people of the Antonio Maceo Brigade, many of them intimate friends, I have lived imaginary fragments of how it could have been. They have lent me, without knowing it, their experiences, their initial frustrations with language, their clashes with such a different culture, and, at times, aggressive. I can *see* myself living in New York, Chicago, Miami, but I don't *find* myself in any one of those places, because I always take with me my true memories, the real ones, the ones I have lived, and I can't, as much as I try, recreate a life that never happened, nor can I imagine my emotions, my intimate ones, in language other than Spanish. I think then about my grandmother, Berta, and her lifelong nostalgia, her yearning, her sadness, and I repeat what I heard her say so many nights, so many times: "I wonder, I wonder."

Notes

1. Casal, Lourdes. 1981. *Palabras juntan revolución*. La Habana: Casa de las Américas; English translation by David Frye, *Bridges to Cuba/Puentes a Cuba* (Ann Arbor: University of Michigan Press, 1995).

2. José Lezama Lima, a part of the group *Orígenes*, was fond of this phrase.

8

La Salida: The Departure

Mirta Ojito

THE POLICE came just as I sat down to lunch: a plain yogurt (sweetened with several spoonfuls of sugar) and an egg sandwich (a fried egg, a little ketchup, bread and voilá!—the Cuban *pan con bistec* of the 1970s). I was wearing half of my school uniform, that is, I had on the painstakingly ironed blue skirt with the two white stripes, signaling I was now in eleventh grade, but on top, I wore a *bata de casa* (a robe for Cuban girls) because I did not want to stain my starched white poplin uniform blouse.

I was just folding the pleats of my skirt over the back of my thighs in the manner nice girls do before they sit down when I heard the steps on the stairs. They were heavy, loud: One, two; one, two; one, one, two. I could tell there were two men and a heavy woman. The woman was easy to identify. She was *"la presidenta del comité"* (the president of the neighborhood watchdog committee) and our downstairs neighbor. Years of listening to people climb the sixteen polished steps that led to our apartment had trained my ear for the idiosyncrasies of their feet. I could tell the men were agile and in charge. They skipped several steps and were at the door before I could call for my mother.

A knock.

I looked at my mother, who was just coming out of the bedroom, where she had been sewing a dress for one of her clients. I waited for a signal from her. She had been waiting for this knock on the door for a long time but I, only for the past 14 days.

It all started the morning of April 24, 1980. I woke up to the sound of my aunt's crying. She was standing at the foot of my bed, looking down at me and muffling her cries with the palm of her hand.

"¿Qué pasa?" I asked, in a panic.

My aunt lived in Guanabacoa, far from our Santos Suárez apartment. She had two small children and a husband. It was still dark outside. What was she doing in our house at this hour, crying at my bed? My sister slept soundly next to me. We had shared the old *sofacama* in the living room since she left the crib at age three, eight years before. She still slept in the inside, next to the wall, protected from falls and other dangers of the night.

"You are going to *el norte*," my aunt sobbed. My mother had joined her.

I could hear them, but I could not see them. The day before I had gone to the ophthalmologist to get my eyes checked, and he had given me eye drops to dilate my pupils. I was to return to his office the following day. So, this is how I woke up the morning I learned I was leaving Cuba, confused and blinded by my very large pupils.

Here's what happened while I slept.

Encouraged by a small announcement published in the newspaper the day before, my father had gone to the old telephone company in Old Havana—the only place where Cubans without telephones could still make international calls—to contact his brother in Hialeah, Florida. The newspaper item, too short to carry a byline, said that boats full of Miami Cubans were heading to Cuba and that anybody who wanted to leave the country in those boats could do so. Not quite believing the story, but hopeful that, for once, he was wrong, my father had to call his brother.

To his surprise, by the time he had arrived at the telephone company on the evening of April 23, there was a long line of Cubans, desperate like him, clutching the same paper. His turn at the telephone came sometime during the night, but nobody

Illustration 8.1. The author in Cuba, 1978

answered at my uncle's house. My father then called his sister. "The reason you couldn't reach our brother," my aunt told him, "is because he has already left for Key West to charter a boat and get you out of Cuba."

Thinking that our departure was imminent, my father rushed home and told my mother, who then called my aunt, our closest relative and the only one who lived in Havana. She came over before dawn to say goodbye and pick up a few things we did not want to leave behind.

And that's when I woke up. And when I heard the story, I immediately thought that April 24 would be my last day in Cuba.

It wasn't.

The police did not come until May 7.

We heard the knock on the door but did not move. Then, our neighbor spoke. "Mirta," she called out to my mother, "*Abre, que es la policía, que ya se van.*" ("Open up. It's the police. You are leaving.")

My mother opened the door. A burly officer, unshaven and dressed in olive-green pants and a white T-shirt, walked in. Without introducing himself, he read our names aloud:

"Orestes Maximino Ojito Denis, Mirta Hilaria Muñoz Quintana, Mirta Arely Ojito Muñoz, y Mabel Ojito Muñoz. Are these the names of the people who live here?" he asked.

My mother, who had started to shake, whispered, "Yes."

He said we were leaving. He also said he needed to do an inventory of the house. My mother told him my father had just left for work. If they hurried, she added, they could probably still find him at the bus stop. My sister was in school. The family had to be gathered and readied. He gave us ten minutes.

Another officer went with my mother to find my father. The burly one stayed behind, poking his nose at every drawer, cabinet, and shelf in the house. I went to the bathroom to change, while our neighbor stood by the door, supervising the scene and making a mental note of the things she wanted to keep for herself.

As I gathered what I wanted to take with me—a tear-smeared handkerchief, a wilting rose, a picture, a letter, a small calendar with a picture of Varadero Beach, a chocolate-colored lipstick, and two pens—I heard the conversation between the officer and our neighbor.

"Why don't you call the other neighbors and arrange something for these people?" He asked her.

He was talking about an *acto de repudio* (act of repudiation), the kind of mini-riot—and sometimes large riot—organized and carried out by neighborhood committees for practically every person who was leaving the country through the Mariel boat lift.

In 1980, the country turned against itself for the first time since the beginning of Fidel Castro's regime in 1959. Neighbors turned against neighbors to harass and torment them for their decision to leave the country. It went something like this: When word got out that someone was leaving, block leaders called on the rest of the residents to stand in front of the house of the person who wanted to leave. They stood there for hours, sometimes days, yelling epithets and throwing rocks and tomatoes at the house. Sometimes windows were shattered; sometimes doors were pushed down; sometimes people were killed; sometimes people killed themselves, trapped inside their homes.

This is what the officer wanted for us.

Our neighbor, a woman who had fought with Castro's guerrillas in the Sierra Maestra mountains, who held the rank of lieutenant and was married to an army colonel, looked the officer up and down and told him, "Nobody touches this family. I've seen these kids grow up."

And, after identifying herself, she ordered: "Get on a chair and get their pictures from the wall. I want to keep them."

Later, when the officer wasn't looking, she took the portable Soviet radio my parents had given me for my fifteenth birthday and hid it under her ample bosom, underneath her equally ample *bata de casa*. By then, my mother and the other officer had found my father, who then left with the officer to fetch my sister from her sixth grade class just a few blocks away. My mother, returning to the house alone, cried all the way and, faint with emotion, fell on the steps that led to the apartment. Neighbors who went to her help found out what was happening. The small apartment soon filled with friends. To the officers' astonishment, the house had a festive atmosphere, sprinkled with a few tears.

My father and sister came back. My sister was worried because, to protect her from an *acto de repudio* by her peers, my father had told her that my mother was ill and had been taken to the hospital. In the meantime, the officer who was conducting the inventory had discovered that we had plenty of food stored in my house. Rows of cans were lined up on the shelves, meat packed in the freezer, rice and beans stacked in boxes on the kitchen floor. "That's a lot of food," he said. "What else have you got hidden?"

It was a moment of terror. Having things was a crime in Cuba. Nobody else seemed to have anything, so the question became, How did you get whatever you have that nobody else does? One source was the thriving black market. Another was our family in Las Villas, who regularly sent us food from the farm. Most commonly, though, it was my parents' thriftiness. They hoarded food and whatever else they could get their hands on to be prepared for a disaster, a time in which things would get worse than they were already. The officer let it pass, perhaps because our friend from *el comite* was still there.

I stood on the balcony alone and said a mental good-bye to my house, my block, my friends, the view. Then, suddenly, my mother called me. It was time to go.

Nobody took the keys.

Less than half an hour before, I had been getting ready to have lunch. And now, here I was, leaving the house where my parents had lived since they married and where I grew up. The lunch remained untouched on the table. My schoolbooks rested on top of a shelf in the bedroom, where I always left them, away from my little sister's prying fingers. My dolls were carefully arranged on top of the dresser. My underwear was neatly folded in the second drawer from the top. My books were by the bookcase, next to the sofa bed. My parents' 72-piece rainbow-colored wedding china was inside a cabinet. Pictures were on the wall, food in the refrigerator, dirty clothes in the hamper, dry linen hanging on the patio.

A home is a hard place to abandon. Where does one end and the home begin? Are treasured possessions just things?

Are the orange curtains my mother made by the light of a *quinqué* a thing, part of a house, or are they part of my heritage, part of my mother? Are the dolls collected over the year just toys or a testament to an imaginative childhood, a remembrance of countless hours spent pretending to be a Mom? Are my much marked and read books just paper and scrawls, or are they my memory, my intellect? Are pictures just that or are they proof of my life, my past? Can a yellow crystal necklace really be replaced? Is there any way to ever recapture the feeling a mother has when she caresses her child's first outfit? And the lingerie, the green baby doll night-gown my mother wore on her honeymoon—can a Victoria's Secret piece ever take its place? And my father's old radio, the one he rescued from a trashcan and fixed—is it just a piece of junk or is it tangible proof of his ingenuity and good taste? Where can he find a watch just like the one he wore for twenty years? Or the rhythms, the sounds, the smells of a lifetime?

In the police car, on the way to wherever it was the police was taking us, I realized I had left behind *The Catcher in the Rye,* the book I had been reading for the second or third time. I had left it next to my bed to make sure I would not forget to take it. I told my parents that I wanted the car to turn around to take me back to the house. They wouldn't hear of it. It was too risky, too dangerous. No time to go back.

We arrived at a place called Fontán in the early evening of May 7. It was a beach club that used to belong to the rich and now belonged to the workers, and it showed. At some point it must have been grandiose. When I saw it, it was in disarray—peeling paint, broken pathways, untended gardens.

The ocean was in the backyard. Thousands of people crowded together on the sand, waiting, for what we did not know. Where was our boat? Where was my uncle? Sometime during the evening, they called our names thorough loudspeakers, and that was how we learned the name of the boat that would take us to the United States: The Valley Chief. From then on, our names became unimportant. The Valley Chief had become our new identity.

We formed lines by boat names. In our group, there were 36 people. Among them was another family of four, a man who did not remember the face of the brother who had come to rescue him, an old woman and a son, an old couple, a young couple with a baby, and a young childless couple. If a sociologist had wanted an accurate sample of who was leaving Cuba in 1980, our group would have been a good one. We were young, old, black, white, professional, truck and bus driver, student, accountant, gay, and straight.

By nightfall, we had become a commune, looking out for each other and making sure no one strayed too far from the group. By nightfall, also, I began to realize that I was really, truly, finally, leaving Cuba. The realization hit me with great force. I realized then that in the attempt to protect our secret, I had not allowed myself to think about its consequences.

The days between April 1 and May 7 had been long and strange. Because the country was engaged in a *de facto* civil war, we had had to tread carefully. We could not tell anyone we were leaving or change our behavior in any way. Yet we could not be out of the house for long periods of time or go anywhere without telling each other where we could be located. At the same time, although we could not take part in the acts of repudiation, we could not criticize them publicly either for fear of retaliation.

On April 19, we had had a close call.

The government had organized a march in front of the Peruvian Embassy, the site where 10,000 Cubans, desperate to leave the country, had congregated in one weekend seeking asylum after a bus carrying six people had crashed against the embassy's fence. Their bold act was the detonator that set off the Mariel boat lift. The entire country was supposed to march in front of the embassy. We closed our windows and doors, cowered in the bedroom, and made not a sound while neighbor after neighbor came to our door pleading, begging, and ultimately, challenging us to come out. They wanted to make sure our block had full participation in the event. Our plan was to let them assume that we were not home, that perhaps we had already left for the march on our own. It worked. We stayed in the bedroom the entire day.

After that, I was never the same. It was the first time I felt fear in my own country, in my own home. I knew it was time to leave.

Still, not quite a month after that, as I sat on the sands of the Fontán beach, I suddenly had the urge to call my friends and say goodbye. I searched in vain for a telephone inside the building. Then it occurred to me to go outside to a corner pay phone to make the call. It was a crazy idea, I admit, but I must have driven my parents crazy with my pleas, because amazingly, my mother obliged and said she would go with me. Without a pass or a passport, for that matter, we walked out of Fontán, leaving my father and sister behind. Later, I came to realize that during the Mariel months Cuban families had been separated for a host of reasons, including the whim of a security officer or even a door guard, but, at the time, still somewhat innocent to the wave of cruelty enveloping the country, we simply walked out.

We were lucky. An enraged mob did not let us go very far. Halfway down the block, before we could get to the pay phone, one of the many people shouting revolutionary slogans outside the Fontán spotted us and spurred the crowd on: "There they go. That's two of them. Let's get them." My mother and I ran back as fast as we could.

Later, I realized the episode had been a fittingly sad ending to my life in Cuba, one that allowed me to make a quicker transition to my new life in exile. Once you have to run from a mob of your own people, it is time to leave—without regrets.

As night fell, my mother and sister found a thin mattress and a space on the floor and went to sleep. My father and I sat in plastic beach chairs in front of them. All night, names of vessels were called over the loudspeakers, a sign that the boat was ready and the group of passengers needed to assemble fast. After the names were called, the people were interviewed by half a dozen uniformed and plainclothes officers at several long, cafeteria-style tables. If everything was in order, they boarded a bus and were taken away. There were no boats on the beach, so we assumed they were shuttled to the port. Nobody ever took the time to explain to us exactly how the process worked or how long it would take.

We did not speak much that night, my father and I, but we observed, and what we saw was pitiful. A grown man, a chemistry professor from Santiago de Cuba, was on his knees, begging an officer to let him join his wife and children who were already in the bus. Her name had been called, but his, inexplicably, had been omitted. When the officer refused to let him go, the wife said she wanted to stay with him to avoid dividing the family. The officer said no to that, too. She must go. He had to stay. And stay he did, crying on his knees, two centimeters from the officer's boots.

There was also an old woman who cried inconsolably because her only son was not allowed to leave with her. Her sister had claimed them both, but, because his name had been misspelled in some document, he was not allowed to go. She, too, wanted to stay, but she, too, was pushed back into the arms of an officer who took her away as she kicked and screamed for her son. The son left quickly, while the chemistry professor still sobbed.

During the crazy months of the Mariel boat lift, more than 125,000 people left Cuba. Many more, an untold number, wanted to leave, but either they could not find a way or were not allowed. I do not think the government purposely set out to divide families; I think it just did not care. It was as if all the hatred accumulated in the twenty-one years that Fidel Castro had been in power had spilled out in one huge wave of suffering. And thus, surrounded by such ugliness and desperation, our first day away from home ended.

Morning found us in the same chairs. We took a walk and ate a little: white rice and a pallid fried egg sprinkled with ketchup. At about noontime, our boat was called. We went through the process without any problems and soon we were sitting in a windowless bus. The windows were there, actually, but the glasses were gone, leaving us exposed to the fury of the mob outside.

As we left Fontán, we ducked, not certain of what to expect. Those who did not were pelted with tomatoes and eggs thrown by the furious mob that waited outside. Some people cried. Others cursed under their breaths. An old lady prayed.

After a short ride, we were in El Mosquito, our next, but thankfully, not our final stop. We formed a long line in the midst of a woodsy, rocky area. Surrounded by tall trees that offered a respite from the unrelenting sun, we waited our turn. What we were waiting for we did not know, but because Cubans were trained to wait in line everywhere, often without knowledge of what was available, we obeyed. Soon it became apparent that what awaited us was not pleasant.

People were taken, one by one, inside a little house with a green roof. There they were interviewed, their papers were reviewed, and they were strip-searched. We had already turned in our identification papers in El Fontán. El Mosquito was the final stop to strip us of our identity and remaining possessions. If something questionable was found during the search, the person was taken away through a side door that we could clearly see from where we were standing in line. At one point, we heard the agonizing screams of one young man who minutes before had been standing before us. We did not see him go out through any door. I assumed there were holding cells inside the house.

While we waited, we wondered what could have triggered the ire of the searchers. Did we have anything on us that could harm our chances of leaving? Could we too be beaten at the whim of an officer? What sets them off? My parents did not say a word. They did not have to. We knew our best hope was to say nothing, to ask nothing, to move through the line and complete the process as smoothly as possible.

Our turn came. Someone asked my name and what I was carrying. I showed him my possessions. He took the two pens, which my uncle had brought from the United States the year before, and sent me to a little booth with a curtain. A woman asked me to take off my pants and panties. Midway through the process she must have realized that I was not hiding anything, and, mercifully, let me go.

Unknown to us, my little sister, who went through the same process, had a plastic bag hidden in her underwear. It contained a picture of our grandfather and a letter that our downstairs neighbor, who loved her like a granddaughter, had sent her from the Soviet Union, where he had gone years before to train for six months. The officer let my sister keep her things.

My father turned in the last of his possessions: $200. He protested somewhat but was told that, where he was going, he would not need Cuban pesos. We emerged from the house without money or identity, not quite sure of what to expect next. What came next was an olive-green tent with no walls. Inside, there were two rows of olive-green bunk beds. Ours was just one of dozens of tents that dotted what turned out to a pretty stretch of beach. The word was that this was the last stop before Mariel. There we met people who had been waiting for their turn to leave for 10 days. We could not fathom spending a day there, let alone a week.

Picture this: We had no towels, no sheets, no clean underwear, or extra clothes. We had not taken a shower or brushed our teeth since we left our house the day before. We had not slept on a bed or taken off our shoes or had a minute alone. We also had not gone to the bathroom.

Someone pointed to a cluster of tents in the distance and said those were the showers and toilets for women. We marched in and quickly came out. The stench was unbearable. Mounds of excrement lined the halls. Flies swarmed around. My mother felt ill. We decided, instead, to take a bath in the ocean. Salt water, we thought, would be better than no water at all, but an officer told us that swimming was not allowed. We went back to the tent.

The food had arrived. Quickly, a line formed, and we dutifully followed. Soldiers handed out little boxes of food. I was so hungry I opened mine right in front of the officer. It was white rice and a boiled egg—except the rice was sort of yellowish and hard and the egg was green. I was so angry I dropped the box. It spilled on the officer's boots. I was lucky, though. He did not even flinch and kept handing out boxes.

The camp was divided in three sections. One large area was reserved for people like us who had been claimed by relatives who had come from Miami in boats. Another area, fenced by barbwire, was for people who had been in the Peruvian Embassy. They had no tents or cots. The third area, closer to the water, was for people who had walked into police stations across the country, declared themselves an *escoria* (scum)—which in Cuba could be anything from a homosexual to an intellectual—and asked for a permit to leave. Those people were also fenced in and guarded by dogs.

The night was fast approaching. We had been told that the loudspeakers continued blaring during the night. If you missed the moment they called out your name, that was it. You had to wait for space on another boat. Nobody knew when. We needed a plan. Accustomed to the neighborhood watchdog committees, we assembled around one bunk bed and decided to break the night into seven shifts, one hour each. The head of each family would stay awake to listen for the name of our boat. Once agreed, we each took a bed. The breeze from the ocean cooled the tent, but the loudspeakers went on, and a spotlight canvassed the entire camp. I do not think anybody in our group slept that night.

In the morning, unexpectedly, our boat was called. "Valley Chief, Valley Chief, Valley Chief." Three times. We rushed to an

Illustration 8.2. The author in Miami, 1980

area where once again we were ordered to form a line. This time, no unpleasant surprises awaited us outside as we rode in a bus to our final stop in Cuba. From the bus, we could see the masts of the boats and ships. We were already at Mariel Port. There were recreational yachts, shrimp boats, and fast sporty numbers hardly big enough to fit two persons. Good Samaritans were throwing apples and little shiny bags from boat to boat. I later learned the bags contained potato chips. I remember thinking it was the first time I had seen apples, but, somehow, I knew what they were. At the time, they represented my future.

There was an atmosphere of buoyancy around the boats. People were coming and going, officers carrying bottles of water, and reporters interviewing refugees and boat owners. As we left the bus, I caught a glimpse of my uncle in the distance—dirty, with a beard from 17 days out at sea. He was wearing jeans and a white T-shirt that contrasted sharply with his suntanned skin. He waved at us.

Behind him, white and motionless, waited the boat that would take us to the United States.

9

The Recurring Dream
Carmen Díaz

Vocation

"WHAT do you want to be when you grow up?"

Answers to this question by children with more or less well-integrated egos are generally influenced by family or social pressures, motivated by a relatively genuine vocational inclination, or the products of the blessed and free flight of their fantasies. In my case, when I understood a first approximation of the various human occupations, I answered with a single word, as imprecise as it was grandiose: científico, scientist, confusing its gender because I could not even be sure that such a profession existed in the feminine gender. My identity happily grew to ripeness when I discovered that there had once been a Polish woman with a French name whom the horrors of life had allowed to teach in the university and whom the horrors of war had allowed to help human beings with her practice and her science. I would be a científica.

The young people of my country, and those of my city in particular, had access in the decades of the 1960s and 1970s to navigable streams of literature, information, and culture in general. We were privileged regardless of social extraction, be it from an impoverished tenement in Pueblo Nuevo or from a luxury condo in El Vedado. Living in the heart of Havana meant having access to the theater, film, ballet, museums, galleries of art, symphony, expositions, and a multitude of publications (many of them reproduced on terrible newsprint that fell apart on the first or second reading), as well as a constant bombardment of ideological education in the Marxist style. The world trembled from student revolts, napalm "that burns, burns, burns" in Southeast Asia, and guerrilla wars in every corner of the Third World. "Create one, two, three, many Vietnams. . . ." I devoured Balzac, Tolstoy, Pirandello, and Galdós. I slept, literally, with the poems of Vallejo, Cernuda, and Nazim Hikmet under my pillow. I learned to love Baroque music and the folk music of Latin America: Quena and flute; the milonga, the valsecito, samba, zamba, chamamé; the Bachianas of today and the moving organ music of yesterday's Bachianas; the "Ospetale de la Pieta" and the "Mozarterium." And secretly, so as not to raise suspicions of "ideological diversionism," I memorized every line of "Sergeant Pepper's Lonely Heart's Club Band" by the boys from Liverpool: "I read the news today, oh boy. . . ." I would have loved, secretly, to perform Mariana Pineda or Yerma. I would have loved, secretly, to travel the world distributing love, as in Tagore's *The Gardener*. I would have loved, secretly and with such passion, to have joined the guerrillas. I would be a guerrillera.

Dear Carlos

You were a blond boy who visited your aunt's store near Trillo Park. Neither you nor I nor circumstances could have foreseen that you would leap out of my word processor on this October afternoon in this other country. I followed you, twenty years later. I left. I came. I found out for the first time, through you, that people did leave "for the North," that black well that swallowed up your friends. I also received, some time later, a visa waiver sent by some Catholic nuns.[1] None of this was ever very clear to me. There was that threat of being sent to Russia and coming back in a can.[2] What the devil did *Patria potestad* mean? Probably something terrible. We talked it over next to the statue of Quintín Banderas, but the fact is that the black well didn't swallow me. I was saved.

I stayed in my city, on my balcony, looking at the serious men who read the newspaper and drank café con leche with those little San Francisco rolls in the Café de Manolo, which was so like an old French café that the similarity still moves me today. I stayed, walking in terror down the sidewalk where those glassy-eyed beings would sit and wait for the Seconal, which some unscrupulous pharmacist would sell them. I stayed, became an adolescent, and lived twenty years of revolution. I never went to Russia, and I came to live in a can many years later when I bought a mobile home in South Florida. Peter Pan, Wendy, Tinkerbell, and the pirate are just a stroll through Disney World for me, or they appear in the magic of a Broadway show with Sandy Duncan flying through the air. The pharmacist, your aunt and uncle, and the gentlemen who read the newspapers all died or disappeared into the well. The drug addicts disappeared mysteriously, followed some time later by milk, coffee, and the little rolls. I stayed, living in that tenement in the middle of the city. I stayed, from time to time saying farewell to some friend as if ripping her from my life. I stayed, became a woman, had two daughters, and studied physics, mathematics, and philosophy. I stayed, only to follow you twenty years later through a sea of sharks and tears. We'll probably never see each other again, but I came.

Y de que van, van. Van. Ban. BAN. BANG![3]

My little daughter was born in March 1970. It was my only victory amid many upsets. All my friends were in the sugar harvest, cutting the cane that I had helped plant myself. We had all the hope in the world that that sugar harvest would blast us out of underdevelopment. In those days one spoke of "developing countries" to refer to the wretched nations of the Third World. I was eighteen, and that spring my priorities were to take care of my little girl and to pass the first physics exams, confident that the effort we had all put in would yield "fruit, " and the targeted level of sugar production would be reached.

The Voice of the Americas endlessly repeated its economic analyses, trying to demonstrate the utopian nature of the enterprise. According to these critics of the revolution, the country did not have the resources, the organization, or the infrastructure it would need to produce ten million tons of sugar. What more could you expect from people whose only desire was to destroy everything we had achieved?

Suddenly, photos of some shoeless fishermen detained in the Bahamas set loose the fury of the crowds that converged before the American embassy. In a matter of hours an enormous grandstand was erected, past which each intellectual, each artist, each member of "the living forces of the nation" filed in anger to deliver speeches against the aggressor's imperialism. Ballerinas and poets, musicians and professors, athletes and politicians—the entire nomenclatura, as they would later be called—made it a point of honor to attend.

I walked slowly because I was in overlong convalescence from an adolescent labor and approached the impassioned crowd that screamed, blasphemed, and burned the Stars and Stripes. The passion seemed disproportionate to me and frightening. I thought I recognized something prefabricated in this demonstration of collective anger, but I couldn't figure out what it was. I went back to changing diapers while a record of a Spaniard singing Antonio Machado's poems spun around and around, smoothly, in the tranquility of my room.

It was in this environment, peaceful and intimate, that I heard Fidel.

I was not the only one who cried. Some of my friends, away in the cane fields, cried too. We would have to start all over. Mechanisms perfectly designed to reconstitute a weakened social ego began to repeat the message. We would turn defeat into victory.

Alma Mater in My Memory

You can climb up the fireworks hill from various points in the city. On cheerful days I liked to leap up the staircase under the stern gaze of the Hellenic virgin with the body of a mulatta. On sad days, the steep side slope and the wall where they killed José Antonio rose up inaccessibly. When I was in a hurry, the cross street with broken sidewalks came to the rescue. Here the enormous roots of trees strained above ground to live in this world of students, by all appearances more entertaining than the dark earth. Another path, way over there, began at the foot of an old prison and smoothly ascended, circling the stadium. At noon I would feel the biting sun and at night the island breeze. There was yet another path spiraling up that lapped the hill and its walls and from which narrow, gray streets emerged. Here is where I found the old student boardinghouses transformed into multifamily tenements and a senator's "love nest" turned into a museum of the French Empire, sitting there, timeless and unexpected.

The colonial army used to juggle their pyrotechnics from those heights. Many years later, it became the site for the Royal and Pontifical University of San Jerónimo of Havana, with a modern name and a somewhat eclectic and grandiose architecture, at once Spanish-American and Republican, neocolonial and cultivated. The air was rife with the history of rebels, iconoclasts, and revolutionaries, as well as hallway gossip, talent, boredom, and contemporary purges to preserve ideological purity of what pretends to be a monolithic order.

Is it possible to love places as you do people? If it were, that hill would be my great love. My friends were the owls and the sparrows that hide in the rafters and even in the great bronze busts hollowed out by time. My loves were the clouds, the marble, and the inspiration. Their ghosts have followed me to this other side of the sea.

The Far Side of the Moon

I left because that world became too narrow for me. It wasn't the way they described it, nor the way I dreamed it. It was an illusion that had been pounded endlessly into our minds, a diabolical and dangerous option that held no options, false rhetoric that washed my brain again and again until it was left empty. I ran out of space. It contracted, as if I'd been moving at the speed of light.

I was terrified and confused. They changed the rules so quickly that only an agile chameleon could have survived. Suddenly, *gusanos* became butterflies who smelled nice, who were joyful and generous and friendly. Suddenly, walking around the city hand in hand with someone who was trying to show me the far side of the moon, I discovered an underworld that I hadn't believed existed. Here the people who played the numbers in Regla placed their bets against the lottery in Caracas, the merchant marines smoked marijuana on the docks, and the foreigners' whores were quick to gossip about when affluent Arabs, Canadians, or Swedes would arrive with a hunger for flesh. Was the implacable persecution of homosexuals, the distressing religious discrimination, and the deep affliction of men, who appear to be human beings, coming out of the political prisons all a bad dream?

The verses of Leninist humor by a poet expelled from the kingdom some time back acquired new flair: "One step forward and two steps back, but always with applause." No, it wasn't my nature to live like a chameleon. I had lost faith, as if we were talking about true believers. I had to leave paradise.

Expulsion of the Heretics

"Scum! Scum! Scum! Scum! Scum!"

"Your name, citizen!"

"Carmen Díaz."

"Tell me your full name!"

"Carmen Bárbara Díaz Machado."

"Reason for leaving."

"I am a prostitute."

"Really? You don't look like a prostitute!"

"I am also a lesbian."

"A lesbian? Are you passive or active?"

"I don't understand what that means."

"Are you butch or femme, chica?"

"Write down both."

"What you are is shameless! Take your safe-conduct and get out, because you're never coming back here again!"

Indiantown

A cold fog that drenched my soul and bones greeted me on the airplane ramp at the Harrisburg airport. I tried to get a mental fix on our geographical location. The passengers, dirty, tired, all but fainting, had seen the peculiar geometry of nuclear reactors file by beneath their windows; they seemed to be those of Three Mile Island, where a few months before a nuclear meltdown had threat-

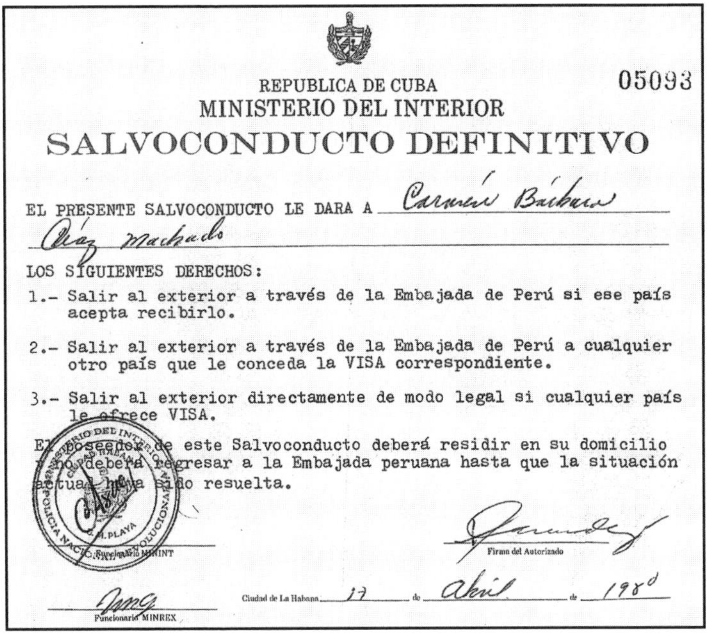

REPUBLICA DE CUBA 05093

MINISTERIO DEL INTERIOR

SALVOCONDUCTO DEFINITIVO

EL PRESENTE SALVOCONDUCTO LE DARA A Carmen Bárbara Díaz Machado

LOS SIGUIENTES DERECHOS:

1.- Salir al exterior a través de la Embajada de Perú si ese país acepta recibirlo.

2.- Salir al exterior a través de la Embajada de Perú a cualquier otro país que le conceda la VISA correspondiente.

3.- Salir al exterior directamente de modo legal si cualquier país le ofrece VISA.

El poseedor de este Salvoconducto deberá residir en su domicilio y no deberá regresar a la Embajada peruana hasta que la situación actual haya sido resuelta.

Funcionario MININT

Firma del Autorizado

Funcionario MINREX

Ciudad de La Habana 17 de abril de 1980

Illustration 9.1. Salvo Conducta (Pass)

ened. A tall military officer, completely blond and smartly uniformed, delivered a welcoming speech, while a Puerto Rican
translator, jovial and mediating, made communication possible:
"Welcome to these United States of America. We shall offer support to those who, like you, have thirsted for freedom. Now you
will go live in an army fort that has been specially conditioned to
receive you. There you will eat and rest. We have arranged for a
bilingual staff to help you. This place has been the home of thousands of Vietnamese refugees who, like you, arrived in this country in flight from communism. We only hope your cooperation
will make the processing shorter. Welcome."

We were coming out of a lethargy of almost three hours of
softly rocking back and forth among the clouds. We had survived
the harsh jostling by the swells of the Gulf amid vomit and tears,
packed tightly together, numb and thirsty, on secondhand slavers'
boats. My fellow travelers had come from jails and sanatoriums,
from marginal neighborhoods, from the temples of Jehovah and
of the Seventh Day Adventists, from unknown corners. I never
thought such as they would be my companions on my first trip
abroad.

Now we were to be called entrants, a substitution for the den-
igrating and shameful epithet we had received in the baptismal
font back there: escoria—scum, slag, a byproduct of steel
foundries that, in this case, could feel and suffer. We felt cold,
hunger, sadness, thirst, nostalgia, joy, love, anguish, and fear.

There were the Blue Mountains in the morning mist and the
windows of the barracks where other refugees had written their
sad stories. The inscription carved in wood should read: "Here
lived Nguyen, left all alone by war." There were the barracks of
single women where one heard the prattle of the lesbians and of
the "females through and through." An apple was brought from
the dining hall and left for Chango on top of an army locker.

Alicia was eighteen unflourishing years old, tattooed with betraying intimacy, burnt by flaming oil from a shipwreck in the
Gulf. Alicia came from prison, where she was sent for practicing

the magic of Lesbos. When she smiled, her grin was devoid of teeth, schooling, and hope.

". . . In Cuba, homosexuals are neither harassed nor persecuted. . . ."[4]

I thought of Puccini's opera *Manon Lescaut* and of my little daughters. We would be back together in a few months, I was sure.

Mamita, Don't Go

I got used to talking to myself or, perhaps, to my ghosts. I couldn't stand not having my daughters with me. I'd be driving the car and holding a conversation with them and explaining everything as if they couldn't see. I lived on this street called Del Rubio, which cut through the city from south to north like a rainbow would cut a cloud. Le Jeune starts by the sea, in a residential neighborhood of spectacular mansions. Some people call it Cocoplum, casting doubt on the origins of some of its inhabitants, tied to who knows what foreign cartels. Here the nouveau rich mingle with another, older Cuban lineage, and even Havana's queen of oils and shampoos spent her afternoons here with her old friends. If there had been as many sugar plantations in Cuba as there were planters in Miami, our country would have been richer than all of Europe put together. The main entrance door opens onto a little plaza where a pair of enormous bronze shoes stands in memory of a Colombian poet.

"You'd love to play here, *mi hijita*. The flowers are so beautiful."

The street narrows then, under the shade of the trees, and then it's reborn with urban flair in a town that names its streets with dubious Castilian spelling.

"I recall one day when you acted up in nursery school and the attendant told you, 'You just git ready for when your mama comes.' You answered her, full of pride, 'You just 'git' ready for when my mama comes and finds out that you said git!' We'll have so much to laugh about."

When I arrived, there were still Americans living there who hadn't folded in the flag and escaped north. Up to a short time ago, membership in this city's golf club was reserved for whites only. This is Coral Gables, a beautiful neighborhood in Miami that doesn't resemble any little town in Spain in spite of all its founders' efforts. Over here, the car salesmen spoil the ambience with their mundane airs, and farther north there's the international airport, where they say a plane takes off or lands every minute.

The people I saw on the corners were the Marielitos, my traveling companions, selling oranges, lemons, mamoncillos, and tomatoes. You couldn't mistake them, with their jeans, their tennis shoes, and baseball caps. Now and then you'd see one of them wearing a gilded Caridad del Cobre around his neck.

Seeking its way north, the avenue becomes like a needle worker as it weaves into another "city of progress," in the style of Marianao during the Republic. That is where the enclave seethes, and only Spanish is spoken. That is where people "gotta sweat in the factory, all because of Fidel," where nostalgia is cultivated. Later, the avenue is split by a little airport, old abandoned hangars, and even an African-American university, where I taught physics and mathematics. Despite the racial disturbances that exploded when we arrived, I felt protected there. My English was "broken," but with numbers and symbols we achieved marvels of communication.

Around there the city is African-American, and the streets of poor and unkempt houses have come out of the The Arabian Nights: Scheherazade, Sinbad, Ali Baba.[5] The forty thieves wandered the streets of this town. At last, the avenue gets lost in an "integrated" neighborhood, shared by Cubans, Dominicans, African-Americans, and Puerto Ricans. On Saturdays they have bembés and toques de santo. The African orishas live in the workers' houses.

I was talking to you, talking to you, talking to you. And at night I dreamed of you. It was always the same dream. Again and again

Illustration 9.2. The author and a daughter in Cuba, 1971

we say goodbye, sometimes on the train platform, sometimes on the bank of some river. It's always the same. You two are hand in hand and get farther away. I hear your voice in the distance.

The Hard Work of Exile

On May 20, 1985, Radio Martí went on the air, and with that, all my hopes for a reencounter came crashing down. The Cubans on the island interpreted it as a violation of national sovereignty, and retaliation was not long in coming. Flights were interrupted, and all attempts at family reunification were obstructed. A tortuous process of selling visas and exit permits began. Phantom agencies appeared and disappeared by magic in Miami. There was a company in Havana that took care of the paperwork. A doctor might cost $10 thousand; two little girls, as much as $15 thousand. Some Latin American governments took part in the business. The visa industry flourished.

I certainly wanted information to reach Cuba unimpeded, but it occurred to me that the impartial press is a joke in bad taste, anywhere in the world. Besides, they should have called it Radio George Washington or Radio Abraham Lincoln. There was a Cuban organization behind all this. A certain Jorge Mas Canosa was spoken of as a kind of American miracle. It was said that he became a successful man by putting up telephone posts. It seemed to me that this puzzle was missing a lot of pieces.

At the same time, I was collecting lost pieces from another puzzle that I hadn't even started to put together yet. The workers in the Gdansk shipyards had rebelled against the workers' and peasants' state. The Pope and President Reagan had become great friends. They said that the standard of living in Cuba had improved slightly and that people seemed more contented. Artistic creativity had flourished a little. New spaces opened. The war in Central America turned bloody and devastating. Cuban doctors were at work in every corner of Nicaragua, while the army harvested victories and death in Angola. Miami appeared to be a strange city where people viewed anything you said with distrust if it was not colored by visceral anti-communism. I learned to keep my mouth shut. I learned to hear behind my back: "Watch out for her. She was trained by Castro." I spent hours playing the "counterpart game" in my mind, in which every character, every event, even every house had a counterpart on the other side of the sea: proton, antiproton; matter, antimatter; the witch on the Comité in Havana, the Miami lady who called me a Castro agent when she heard me talk about South African apartheid. Each one had a partner. We were all the same, here and there, incapable, up to then, of accepting otherness.

My dear little sister, I've made the arrangements through Panama with the man that Mami sent me. He says that if it's not through Panama, it'll be through Costa Rica. He looks like a crook, but I gave him the money because you have all insisted that this is going to get "resolved." We'll be together again soon. I love you. Give my little girls a kiss.

—Carmen

Comité

Someday I'm going to publish a guide to exile community political organizations. It'll list each group's name and address, which may turn out to be a post office box, and a brief history recounting the day it was formed, probably from the break-up of a previously existing organization. Multiple mitoses. It'll be an enormous volume, attesting to our historical incapacity for negotiation, alliances, pacts, and timely and efficient civility.

Tired of waiting, emotionally drained by absence, with the help of new friends I worked to form a committee to mobilize some social forces behind family reunification. I couldn't know that from that point on, I would always be struggling within a committee.

The stagnation and political manipulation of the governments of Cuba and the United States, who played the immigration question like a game of ping pong without paying much attention to how they were tearing people apart, were costing me my life. Time is irretrievable. I'll never be able to be with my daughters all the time that I wasn't there. My attempts to bring over my little sister never bore fruit. The "bad man" disappeared with the money, and my sister, at nineteen years of age, for this and many other reasons, decided to leave not only Cuba but also the world itself. How much pain can a human being endure? An infinite amount, it seems.

The name of my committee had more words in it than there are members in its governing board. We Cubans are so grandiose. I started to play the political game. I learned what "checks and balances" really meant and how to be and not be "politically correct." I discovered Congress, local politicians, Spanish language radio. I got hundreds of letters from other Cubans torn apart by separation and by the injustice that our cruel histories reproduced. My new friends from the traditional Left were my treasure. What a screwed-up people we were. My God!

The Marazul plane headed into the sky. Around us were blue sea and blue sky, with a brilliant green strip in the middle. The

Illustration 9.3. The author, her daughters, and her sister at Havana's el malecón, 1973

island was so narrow, as if it really were a caiman. The men on the ground were Lilliputians, scrambling over its rugged skin. Music started up in a whisper like tinkling bells. It was an intimate Dialog that I hadn't heard for nearly ten years. It was a merry music of innocence that Mozart or Vivaldi would have envied. I was leaving Cuba again, but this time with a valuable cargo. On another seat, in front of mine, the girls were prattling in their adolescent language. I was leaving Cuba again, to return many times. To return, I think, always.

Notes

1. Through the Catholic Church visa wavers were distributed to unaccompanied minors.

2. One of the rumors that fueled the exodus of unaccompanied children in the 1960s was that children would be sent to the Soviet Union and packed in cans.

3. The campaign to harvest 10 million tons of sugar and the origins of the name of the musical group, Los Van Van.

4. Editorial, *Granma*, official newspaper of the Communist Party of Cuba, April 1980, p. 2.

5. Burton, Richard, trans. 1934. *The Arabian Nights Entertainment: The Book of the Thousand Nights and a Night.* New York: Heritage Press.

10

Only Fragments of Memory
Raquel Mendieta Costa

First Impression

I VIVIDLY remember the morning of January 1, 1959. It was unusually early when I heard cries of "Batista has fallen!" "The tyrant is gone!" At first I thought I was dreaming, but immediately afterwards I heard my grandmother knock on my parent's bedroom door, and I heard them getting out of bed while talking excitedly in muted tones, trying not to waken my brother and me.

The whole house got up, and my parents decided to set out immediately for Havana to await the arrival of "the rebels." I begged them to take me, but they said no, they wouldn't have time to take care of children. In less than an hour they were gone.

I felt totally disillusioned. We had been waiting so long for the triumph of the rebels that it seemed unbelievable to me that they would leave me out of what I somehow recognized, in my early, seven-year-old consciousness, as the birth of a new era.

Later on, about noontime, my grandmother saw a man go by with a July 26 armband. Grandpa, Grandma, Isa, and Manuela peered out cautiously from the windows of my parent's bedroom. They didn't let us children get close, as if some dangerous person were patrolling the house. A few moments later Manuela broke out laughing, and said, " Don't worry, Señora, it's just Luisito Chacho, the gardener's assistant."

We returned to Havana after Fidel had already entered the city. Everything seemed completely changed. I remember the emotion when, coming out of the tunnel on Línea Avenue, I saw my first rebel. Although he didn't look like much—a thin man with a rustic appearance, dressed in a faded, olive-drab uniform and sporting long hair and a beard, which was utterly unusual at that time—he was beyond a doubt one of the heroes. You could feel the effervescence in the streets: People walked with unaccustomed energy; children dressed like rebels, down to the fake beards sold from the countless itinerant carts from which hung little olive-drab uniforms, flags, and July 26 armbands. By the time we were at Seventh Avenue I couldn't hold back any longer and I begged my parents to buy me a beard, but my mamá thought it unhygienic, so I had to make do with a July 26th armband.

The Excision

I think that if anything defined the way I looked at the world during the first years of the Revolution, it was amazement, amazement at a world that was radically changing, becoming the opposite of everything I had known up to that point. The people who used to inhabit my life disappeared as if by magic: "They left for the North," we would hear, and we began to speak of them in the past tense, the way you speak of the dead. The world was split in two irreconcilable halves: before and now, there and here, "worms" and revolutionaries, traitors and patriots, Catholics and Communists. Both halves tugged at our hearts, dividing our emotions, our friends, our families, and above all else, forcing us to decide.

My Grandparents

The last time I saw them was when I went with them to Santa Elvira. It was the same little church where, on December 24, I used to hurriedly kiss the feet of the image of the Christ child, trying to shorten the time that remained before we could untie the presents decorating the great pine that served as the Christmas tree. From Fulano for Mengano, from Sutanejo for Esperancejo, sang my aunt's voice, while some of us enthusiastically opened one present after another in succession, and the rest of us waited and hoped, anxious and entertained, that ours would be coming, too.

But this time it was different. I hadn't seen them in months, and they asked me to accompany them to Mass. My grandfather was old, tired; his criollo sense of humor had developed into an acerbic and skeptical irony. Now he spent most of his day sitting in the doorway of his house, contemplating the sea with a worried look I had never seen on him before while he smoked, one after another, the cigarettes that had come to replace his eternal H. Upmman #2 cigars. People who passed by on the way to the beach would greet him:

"Good morning, Virgilio, how are you?"

"Sitting here, hoping I die before I run out of money," was his unvarying reply.

He dedicated his nights to listening to La Voz de las América, or any other radio station that held out the hope that the nightmare he was living would end at some point.

My grandmother, however, kept the air of a cavalry sergeant, despite the cerebral hemorrhage she had suffered three years earlier upon learning that they had lost, on the fatal day when they changed the currency, all the money my grandfather had saved his whole fifty years of working and that the world of securities and well-being they had managed to put together with such effort was collapsing irreparably.

As I entered Santa Elvira Church, I ran into the same thick quality in the air that I could sense in my grandparents' house, but here it became profound, dense, almost compact. There were mostly old people in the church; you scarcely saw a child or adolescent at Mass. Some had stopped going as a consequence of the conflict between the Church and the Revolution, and others were in the refuge of Miami as a result of the political campaign over *patria potestad*. The hymn rang out, "You will reign, O blessed

King," up to the climactic lines of "may your heart reign / in our land and on our soil. / Our nation is of Mary"; it was less an act of faith than a political challenge to the Revolution. And I, standing there, next to my grandparents, felt that this fervent and collective song was little more than a last, long, brazen lament for a world collapsing irreparably, feeling that, in spite of my mere twelve years of age, I had to choose. It was like the final push, the most painful, the most enlightening. I had at last lost the final tie, and I perceived, with all my senses heightened, life.

Time Taken On

When I saw her go by, hanging onto the side of the truck, I don't know why I recalled the photo taken when we were water skiing: She was in the center, with the grace she had for everything she did, with the natural elegance with which she took on all risks, with the daring that made her so different. In the photo she looked younger than she was: skiing her slalom, erect, leaning back a bit. To the left was my brother, about eight, in a position that gave the sensation of instability. I stood to the right, more aggressive and less elegant than she, in a bathing suit with white and blue stripes that I remember as my favorite.

Now I stood still on the sidewalk, absorbed, remembering those other times so different from these, wondering how she had gotten used to this new life. I realized, though, that for her, everything always took on some special significance; just as much in the past as now, her reality moved in some other dimension. Everything she did was touched by the sign of the extraordinary, and her place could be none other than this: right here, now, in this very instant, where a new world was being born that would be more just.

Those were years of constantly dying and being born again, when everything that had up to then seemed familiar turned strange, unrecognizable, as if it were showing some new face of anguish or of hate. They were the years when the house of my childhood's toys took on a quality I found alien, one that thickened through the whispers of new visitors and only dissipated when my father's loud voice reverberated against the walls, as it did on the afternoon when he told my grandfather:

"Virgilio, if you prefer, we will not visit your house any more. But remember, you have only one daughter, and we are not going north."

My grandfather, in peace at last, sat down to wait for death to come before he ran out of the little bit of money they hadn't taken from him. And he succeeded.

Those were also the years of the great, long speeches that reached us through television. We felt how, in the time between one game that bored us and what it would take us to invent another, The Illusionist constructed his new realities, weaving them with resonant, deep words that spoke to us of hope for that better world.

I remember one of those days in particular: The voice of The Illusionist had been filling space for several hours, and on television we could see a shot of the Plaza of the Revolution with thousands of tiny little points and, among them, one giant sign that stuck out: "With you until we eat malanga," not knowing yet that malangas would come to be a luxury food, and that, directed by my mother and in an act of the most profound patriotism for our young years, my brother and I would sing "The July 26th Anthem" so that, between one verse and the next, we could swallow down spoonfuls of a horrible porridge of boiled split peas.

The fishing trips, the canasta games, and the days of water skiing and underwater expeditions had been replaced by endless lines, militia guards, and productive labor. We no longer had servants in the house to clean and cook. The last one had been Gladys.

Dawn was coming up when the first explosions were heard, and my mother, like a dog that had just given birth, stuck us under the bed. She wasn't afraid, just frightened: by the bullets, by the noise of the machine gun firing from the terrace of the house in front, by the bloody scab on my brother's knee, opened when he threw himself off the bed. Just then Gladys the cook arrived, half-dressed and "butt in the breeze," who on hearing my mother's joke would laugh, like us, with those white teeth she would later exchange for teeth of gold. Afterwards the waiting began: waiting for reports while we played war against "the mercenaries," waiting until we heard that "the invasion has been smashed in less than seventy-two hours." My mother began picking up from all over the house the useless bullets from the two display-case pistols.

And I still stood there, surprised—I don't know why—to see her pass by, hanging from that Russian truck on which she was returning from some productive labor, covered with red earth, one foot on the running board and holding on with both hands to the bracket of the driver's mirror, in the same erect and elegant posture with which she used to begin her days of water skiing in Varadero.

The Beatles Have Ideological Problems

"The Beatles have ideological problems," Llanusa informed me categorically when he called me into his office for a warning, because I had been photographed in the newspaper with one of their records in my hand upon my arrival at the airport from a swimming competition in Germany.[1]

The first song had been "Anna"; my brother had brought it home recorded on a "platter" that, both by looks and by sound, seemed to belong more to an old gramophone than to a stereo turntable. I continued to prefer "La Aragón." Then came the others: "P.S. I Love You," "Close Your Eyes," and "Twist and Shout." By then I was letting my heretical bangs grow, which made me look like Ringo Starr and meant, both in the INDER (National Sports Institute) and in high school, that I must have "ideological problems," too.

That was my first rebellion: From the moment they were prohibited, I gathered my bangs at the high school door with a triumphant hairclip in the middle of my brow. But that wasn't the only prohibition: They forbad "foreignizing" music, miniskirts, jeans, bell-bottoms with zippers in front, large sunglasses, long hair and tight pants for boys, suspicious literature, conversations about UFOs, homosexual relations, letters with the ones who left, relations with foreigners, clergy in the universities, Christmas Eve, your personal truth, individuality, and for a time, even New Year's parties. The prohibitions only succeeded in making us more vehement, however. Those were the magical years of the 1960s, when we all dreamed of being guerrillas, and we all went to the Cinemateca every day and saw the best of the European and Latin American film vanguard at any theater in Havana; read García Márquez, Vargas Llosa, Cortázar, Sartre; attended conferences on history, architecture, literature or film in the Sala Talía or Meme Solís concerts in the Comunidad Hebrea; held passionate discussions about anything while standing in the Sunday afternoon lines to wait for supper at the Carmelo de Calzada or the recently opened pizzeria at 12th and 23rd. We danced at any of the countless parties on Saturday night, because if none of us could offer a house for our own party, we would wander all over El Vedado in groups looking for one we could crash.

Competition

Every goal you have in life is like a 200-meter butterfly competition. The people who are watching from the bleachers merely enjoy the spectacle of a group of swimmers gliding agilely across the water, but the ones who participate in the competition share the anguishing responsibility of being winner or loser. In the last instance, human beings can only be divided into winners and losers, beyond whether you win or lose some competition or other. What makes the difference is that losers, from the moment they take off, do it knowing that they are going to give up in the third lap, the most difficult one, while the winners are going to struggle up to the end; and that is their trump card.

From the moment I heard my name over the loudspeaker, calling me to the starting block, my soul divided into two halves: one that wanted to give up, throw it in before starting, and another that knew it had to prevail, not only against tiredness, psychological pressure, nervousness, and the ability of the other competitors, but above all, against its own other half. I took several deep breaths and jumped into the water to pee the last nervous little stream.

Out again, wet and tense, I felt nausea well up from the depths of my fear. I stood on the starting block and, when I heard the voice say "on your mark," tensed my muscles and concentrated on reaching perfect communion between my mind and my body, with the aim that my head would think each contraction and relaxation of my muscles during the ephemeral and infinite two minutes or so that the event would last.

The first lap was easy. I felt light, strong, agile, full of physical energy. Only for a few instants did I perceive the anguish you get from the knowledge gained in previous experiences, and I tried to block that sensation, consciously ordering my body through each movement, each miniscule gesture.

I tried to arrive at the first 50 meters among the pacesetters, for I knew that each meter, each tenth of a second won against exhaustion was crucial. Only after 75 meters or so did I begin to feel it: an exhaustion that accumulated in my arms, began to keep the air from reaching my lungs with regularity, forced me to speed up my breathing rhythm, and, above all, made my two halves, the winner and the loser, start what was for me the real competition—being able to pass psychologically that point where your whole body, debilitated, is crying out to you to stop, to give up, to forswear achieving something that, at this moment, your losing half will show you is secondary, dispensable, minor, unimportant.

Between 100 and 150 meters was where I won or lost. "Give up, give up," my losing side decreed. The winning side blocked the order by concentrating on every movement: one stroke, another, now kick; breathe once, two strokes now; tense the arms, pull, relax the muscles, tense them again, and pull once more; breathe, pull, kick. At last, the agony ended. When I made the turn for the last 50 meters, I felt that my body, although exhausted, was responding again. My losing side had lost the only battle it would have liked to win, and my arms and legs moved now with the anger you feel when you think that, despite all your effort, you could still lose the competition, while your eyes search, between one stroke and the next, for the faces of the other competitors.

University

I began to study at the School of Letters at the University of Havana in January 1971, right after the failure of the Ten Million Ton Sugar Harvest and at the beginning of the Quinquenio Gris, the Grey Five-Year Period. I remember my years of university study as one of the worst nightmares of my life. I could never recover from the sense of oppression that overcame me every time I climbed the stairs to the entrance to the School of Letters.

Purges were nothing new at Cuban universities, but the First Congress on Education and Culture made them fashionable once again. Nonetheless, the School of Letters did not conduct purges. More sophisticated, they used the structure of the "insertion" system: every student had to be "inserted" into a workplace. For the "marked" ones, the undesirables, or simply those of us who had to fulfill the necessary quota to demonstrate the "revolutionary combativeness and intransigence" of active comrades in the Party or the Juventud, they designed the printing press and the match factory.

Right-left, right-left—my body moved as if rotating over and over again on the same axis, endlessly, interminably, while minutes and hours passed, and the sheets came out of the stitching machine into my hands, and I threw them, like a major league pitcher, to the binders that stood at the table.

That morning, when Rodolfo (whom we called Born Beneath the Cow's Tail) called us together at the door of the printer's to inform us we would no longer be rotating the half hour established for working on the stitcher, that because of my productivity I would, from now on, always be the final, rhythmic, well-oiled, precise, inhuman link in the machine, I understood it was a challenge: the dare—arrogant, imperious, beyond appeal, absolute—came to me from the smiling diarrheic cow's eyes that he hid behind the thick lenses of his glasses. I accepted.

You thought, Rodolfo, that I wouldn't hold out, that I'd give you, at last, a chance to bring me before a School Council and they'd kick me out of the University; but you were wrong, because your problem was how to screw me, and mine was how to survive you. There you kept me, while I passed the minutes and the hours with my best smile and my most insolent look.

At twelve o'clock silence fell and spread to the halls of the University. It must have sounded to you like Cinderella's last waltz, with the difference being that you never had her redeeming slipper because you'll always be one of those many mediocre men with ambitions for power who go through the University without the University ever getting through to them.

That was perhaps what most pained you, and because of that, you preferred to distort everything, to judge us by the "parameters"—that latest little concept you loved to use so much. So that thinking well of a friend, in spite of what you really thought of him or her, meant having a petit bourgeois concept of friendship; or simply disagreeing with what the Juventud decided meant having ideological problems, as if you, like some kind of god, was the ruler of words and thought. So, in the analysis meeting of the Brigade, you told Gloria María she couldn't graduate with Distinction because her grades were too good because of her "academicism," the favorite sin of the Inquisition of the Mediocre.

I remember when we discussed the Social Service Law, and Born Beneath the Cow's Tail first explained to us, between warbling and beating his chest, his obscure bovine origin and that because of it, he felt "obliged to go wherever the Revolution needed him." It seemed, however, that where the Revolution most needed him was in Havana, not in his obscure place of birth, for by his last year in college he had changed the address in his ration book to the house of the old lady who rented him a room and had negotiated for himself one of the best jobs, without letting either of these facts impede his long moralizing speeches in which he judged the "petite bourgeois attitudes of those comrades who seem incapable of repaying the Revolution for all it has done for them."

My generation was by now well schooled in the double standard that had imperceptibly been with us from the very beginning.

Swan Song

They say that the swan sings right when it is about to die. That was the 1980s in Cuba. The decade was framed by the two most blatant axiological crises in the whole process of the Revolution: the events at Mariel and the execution of General Ochoa. Nevertheless, many of us still remember those years with nostalgia, because on the one hand our standard of living grew considerably: The blackouts that had plagued us for more than twenty years all but came to an end, food shortages were down to a minimum, and in the Mercado Central and the mercaditos you could buy everything from chocolate to sausages and ham, not to mention cheese and butter, items that only two or three years earlier we thought we would never eat again. You could get into bars and restaurants without standing on line; public transport was almost regular; you could have hopes of buying a car during your lifetime, or a new refrigerator, or an air conditioner, or even traveling as a tourist to the socialist countries.

On the other hand, the atmosphere of expressive liberality that one began to breathe contrasted sharply with the ideo-aesthetic repression of the previous decade, when they had tried more forcefully than ever before to establish socialist realism as the model for Cuba's artistic and literary world. Now we had conceptual art, postmodernism was being discussed, and literature was turning intimate, even Lezamian.[2]

In any case, we knew—and I speak in the first person plural because I believe this was a general phenomenon of consciousness that concerned both of the younger generations—everything wasn't well, that the country was becoming more and more stratified, and that we were trapped in a Nintendo game over which we had no control. Even so, we believed. We knew that countless things had to change, and we thought that the country's internal politics were going through an irreversible process of flexibility for which we somehow felt responsible. We believed that the errors of the past could never be repeated, that the history we had lived and suffered had to do some good, and that the moment had arrived for us to raise our voices. The crushing proof that we were wrong came with the execution of Ochoa. Nothing could change such a well-established machine. Today you could be a "Hero of the Republic of Cuba" and tomorrow, a traitor.

Puente de Hierro

Who would have said that we would be happily searching through all the newspaper stands of Havana for a copy of *The Moscow News*? Glasnost and perestroika reached us almost without our noticing, imperceptibly but with unexpected force, just at the right moment, when a whole movement of consciousness was starting to gather force in the country, particularly in the artistic and intellectual world.

Things changed quickly. On one July 26 they declared the Special Period, exported artists to Mexico and other countries, silenced the most combative journals, suppressed public transportation almost completely, introduced bicycles, reduced food to a bare-survival minimum, and began the system of daily sixteen-hour blackouts.

Coño, I'm dying of hunger, and I still have to see how I get back home. Good thing the Foundation's[3] at least on Línea, a nice, level street, because if I had to climb the hill up to 23rd I think I would have resigned from this whole journal business by now. And to top it all off, this heat is killing me! I'm so covered with sweat I could wring out my tee shirt. Coño, they gave me a red light! Let me

Illustration 10.1. Kaky and friends in Havana, 1990 (photo by María de los Angeles Torres)

coast so that maybe I won't have to stop. I'm so tired! And not even halfway there yet. When I get to Puente de Hierro I'm going to get off; I don't want to fall. The other day a car ran over a guy who fell. Nereida and Nena are coming today. I don't really understand this documentary they're doing. Bet they'll come by the house tonight and bring rum. Hope they bring something to eat, too, because if they don't I won't be able to take a single swig. In any case, if they call first I'm going to tell them, because it's been more than six months since the last time they came to Cuba, and no matter how much people might have told them, I'm sure they don't have the slightest idea what's going on here. Good thing the bridge is coming up now. When I get to the other side of it, it's almost like I start a countdown of the meters. That guy standing over there with the bag: I bet he's selling peanut bars. I think I have about twenty pesos, so if they haven't raised the price I m going to buy one, because if I don't eat anything I'll never make it back home. The water and sugar I had for breakfast is all used up now. I'd like to know who decided that sugar is fattening: I eat practically half a pound a day, and every day I look more skeletal. Forget it, those aren't peanut bars; the guy's changing dollars. If they catch him they'll split his head. Coño, I'm so hot and so hungry! Forget it— I'm going to have to take a break at Hugo's house. I don't think I even have the strength to climb the hill on 26th Street. I'll take First Avenue, but won't the headwind be too strong? Calm down, Kaky Mendieta, because otherwise you'll have to drag yourself to Hugo's house, and there, even if you re lucky, you'll just get your-self some caña santa tea and nothing else. Coño, we're so screwed over, and the worst thing is that there doesn't seem to be any end to it. I don't know what those people are thinking. How long do they think people can keep going? And to top it all, there's a black-out now, so there won't even be any water at home. How I wish I could just take a bath and get into bed! How tired I am, Coño! And how hungry!

The Most Obscure Object of My Desire

Do you want to know what the worst thing is about this Special Pe-riod? Everything: the tiredness, the blackouts, the boredom, the hunger. For the past three years, once a day, we've eaten the same thing: rice, red beans boiled with caña santa or basil, and biomass. Biomass? Officially it's called "meat mix." Remember the dog meat they used to sell? It's something like that, a lumpy paste; some-times it looks kind of pink, and other times it's gray. You mix it with flour or yuca or anything you can get to toss into it, and you make a kind of mix: biomass. You can make a kind of pancake with it. There isn't any oil, so you throw it onto a griddle and burn it on one side and then the other. The meat mix is indescribable; it doesn't have any recognizable flavor. There's nothing comparable.

You'd have to eat it and taste it—if you can call it tasting—to know what I'm talking about. We've been eating it for the past three years, so our taste buds are now completely virgin, and any new flavor has an incredible intensity. Maybe the new flavor you taste is just spaghetti boiled with salt. We always thought that spaghetti with salt was something horrible, but all of a sudden that flavor has acquired a new dimension: It's a different flavor, because we don't get pasta very often any more, maybe once every six months or once a year. And when you've spent so long eating the same thing all the time, and then you eat something different, it's as if you discover it for the first time in your life—at least, in your conscious life—the virgin taste of things. Our taste buds are virgin taste buds that distinguish flavors in rather the same way a refined musical ear can hear, in a symphony orchestra, when each of the instruments enters: You hear a cymbal crash, the cellos, the violins starting up. That's what happens with taste buds: If you eat something with complex flavors, you can sense how those flavors come entering in, from the most primary to the most complex. What I long for now isn't the salty stuff we used to eat. What I long to eat is a *señorita* (a Lady Finger). If I could eat a *señorita,* I'd get to taste so many different things, like the dough—the puff pastry. In the puff pastry dough I d taste everything, from the primary flavor of the flour and butter it's made with, to the complex flavor of the flaky pastry itself. I'd taste all those primary compositions.

But first, I'd taste the sugar.

No, the sugar goes on top, and the first thing my tongue would touch would be the pastry underneath. The sugar would have to be a very fine, powdered coating, and it would also have many flavors: the sugar itself, the sugar with the flour, the sugar with the butter, the sugar with the pastry that it's covering. And then—then I'd start to enjoy the cream, the cream that the *señorita* has between one layer of puff pastry and the other. Then I'd move on to a more complex flavor that would integrate all these primary flavors, until at last it would turn into the *señorita,* properly speaking. The *señorita* itself.

That's probably the greatest lesson of the Special Period. No, no, man, I'm fooling with you because I'm getting tipsy, but I'm not kidding. It's true, what I'm telling you.

Revelation

What a mess! The plane to Atlanta doesn't leave for seven hours, and I can't find anybody at home. I was hoping that el Coco would be in, but no luck. Just half an hour ago I was in Havana, and now here in Miami, which for me has always been such an alien place and so nearby at the same time, because in the end it is precisely the other side of the same coin.

This time there's something different, worse. It's the strange sensation that I've opened a door to another dimension, another world that we can't even imagine any more. It's not that everything is clean, new, cared-for, or that people speak a mixture of English and Spanish. I think it's the people or the people's attitude. Like all of them know where they're going. I think it's something in the eyes.

People in Havana walk around with their eyes lost, disconcerted. Yes, it's something in the gaze. In Cuba people have a gaze that's empty of any hope. "What's going to happen? What's going to happen?" How many times a day for the past three years have they asked us the same question without our ever being able to answer?

We've turned into a country without any hope, as if we were swimming eternally in some third lap that leads nowhere, because in reality the competition ended long ago. That's it. I feel my whole life has been like swimming an unending third lap, endless because we've been thrown out of the fourth.

I haven't left Cuba in three years, precisely the three years of the Special Period. Maybe that's why I haven't noticed just how much we have deteriorated. I don't feel I have anything to reproach myself for, because I've tried to fight against my spiritual deterioration with all my might. I've tried to rise above all the calamities and adversities of this reality so that what has happened to others wouldn't happen to me. I wouldn't let myself be dragged away by hopelessness, desperation, apathy, and depression, but where has it all gotten me? It's gotten me nowhere, because there's no way to escape this reality. Every road leads to the same point, like an infinite labyrinth with no exit.

And now where?

Notes

1. José Llanusa was the founding president of the National Institute of Sports, Physical Education, and Recreation (INDER) and was named Minister of Education in 1965.

2. The dominant poetic convention in Cuba from the 1960s to the early 1980s was "conversational poetry," an "exterior" poetic form that centered on the problems of man/woman in the social context. In the 1980s Cuban poetry became more intimate and increasingly dealt with spiritual themes, invoking the styles of José Lezama Lima (1910–1976), known for his densely complex, "hermetic" writing.

3. Pablo Milanés Foundation.

11

Words Without Borders
Madelín Cámara

> *To reach the heavens you need one long ladder, and*
> *another short one . . .*
>
> —MERCEDES SOSA,
> "VOLVER A LOS 17"[1]

THE HISTORY of an exile does not begin the day we leave the country, but on the day we feel that the country has abandoned us. What I write has its origins, then, in that process of inner rupture, in the way distance gets accepted as an option, the break-ups that this causes, and finally the imposition of distance in the form of a border, exclusion.

Perhaps I should go back to when I was seventeen, like Mercedes Sosa said in her song, to when I was just about to start at the University of Havana. I remember that my enthusiasm and my tolerance for the Revolution (that's how I classified the opposing feelings I had toward everything from Silvio Rodríguez's songs to the ice cream at Coppelia) were still untouched then.

The School of Letters changed me. Literature opened the world to me, but I also discovered the consequences of envy, opportunism, and the generalized practice of denunciation and blackmailing. What is most painful to recall is that these lessons came from people my own age, my own classmates. The mass youth organizations—the University Student Federation (FEU), which any student who wanted to could join, and the Young Communist Union (UJC), made up solely of party faithful selected for their political loyalty—were excellent instructors in the arts of alienation and dissimulation.

At least in my experience, the collectivist spirit these organizations preached was a means of controlling students' personal and ideological freedom of choice. Because both of them represented "the best of revolutionary youth," we all, absolutely all, had to follow or pretend that we followed the norms they communicated to us in unbearable meetings and monotonous manuals that no one read or wanted to read. In the end, what the process left me with were certain techniques of pretense that allowed me to maintain a precarious balance between not being like them and not falling into disgrace and being considered a *"gusana"* or "antisocial."

First Farewell to Utopias

My marriage to Ralph, a Danish researcher, placed me on the suspicious list. Ralph had come to Cuba to study the works of José Martí. Ralph believed, like a utopian socialist, in a regime of social equality, and he was confident that the Revolution would make that old dream come true—until he was faced with the undeniable evidence of its failure. For both of us, the evidence came with the events at the Peruvian Embassy and the Mariel exodus of 1980. None of us who lived through that apocalypse will ever forget the grotesque and cruel scenes of crowds who beat, cursed, and shouted at anyone who had decided to leave the country upon the government's arbitrary decision to open the doors to everyone who wanted to exit. Statistics say 125,000 people abandoned Cuba in less than two months.

I retain in my memory the mixture of nausea, fear, and shame I felt witnessing those events. Although I never took part in the so-called acts of repudiation, neither did I oppose them with anything more than verbal criticisms, sotto voce. How else?

Illustration 11.1. The author and her daughter in Cuba, 1983

For the two years that followed these episodes, I was unemployed. University officials had refused to grant me an assistant professorship because of my *inmadurez política* (political immaturity), a label still used to classify the unfaithful to the government. Nevertheless, I was happily occupied. I had a daughter, Lena. Ralph wanted to return to his country, but I did not want to follow him to Denmark. Eventually, we were divorced.

Where the Serpent Bites Its Tail

The year 1989 was critical for the world. The social reform processes of glasnost and perestroika, led by Mikhail Gorbachev in the USSR, spilled over into neighboring countries. The Berlin Wall fell in pieces; the KGB archives were opened; Timosoara brought the Romanians to the brink of civil war. The socialist world was coming apart, and the millions who lived under its rule saw the coming of a new era they both feared and desired. Something unstoppable was happening.

The year 1989 was also key for Cubans. The trial of General Ochoa reached me by television in my house in Cojímar. Of course I didn't know who Arnaldo Ochoa was, nor was I aware of the existence of a Department MC of State Security. We ordinary Cubans tend not to know what goes on at the top until one day it proves useful for the leaders to let us in on it, as if we had been accomplices all along and reaping gain from everything that happened. In the end, these were the facts that were put forth: Ochoa and a group of high level army and security officials were accused of having established a powerful network that used international organizations for trafficking in drugs and other goods. Officers formerly decorated as Heroes of the Nation for their deeds in the underground, in the Sierra, in Escambray, and now in Africa, were seated at the defendants' bench and found guilty.

Many thought the trial was an elaborately staged farce aimed at an audience of believers, the 10 million of us watching the TV screen. The trial was unprecedented, and for that reason the punishment was exemplary. Truth had to be reestablished, treason punished, so people once more could believe in their leaders. Everyone can tell it their own way, but I found different results in the Ochoa case. It brought on a true collective catharsis, a massive identification of the people with a group of men who had dared to defy the control of the center—albeit by embezzlement and illegal enrichment—and had demanded their own share from a scheme in which they were thought of as mere instruments. I don't think anyone doubted that those on top were implicated in the drug trafficking and other activities. It was impossible, given the government's control over everything that happens on the island, that anything of the sort could take place without the approval of the high command. That is precisely why it was so disgraceful to see how it was all manipulated to achieve two political objectives: cleaning up the image of the Cuban State abroad and making it very clear inside the country that any attempt at subversion would be severely repressed.

The lesson was obvious. The Grand Tribunal could judge any one of us; it could strip us of our medals, of the car we got this year, even of our lives. Ochoa was shot by firing squad on July 13, 1989, together with Patricio de la Guardia. The others were imprisoned, among them the Minister of the Interior, who died in prison shortly afterwards of a sudden heart attack.

Happiness is a warm gun.—John Lennon[2]

As a consequence of a period of economic recovery, during 1986 to 1989 the cultural institutions in Cuba began to allow some room for debate. Principal among them were the projects Castillo de la Fuerza for the fine arts and Paideia for literature. The first of these turned a former military fortress in Havana, then a museum of weaponry, into an alternative exhibition space for the youngest generation of painters. The conversion of this space was more than symbolic. The works presented there were characterized by a critical discourse on aesthetic and ideological dogmas and included treating with parody the major myths of the Revolution, from Martí to Fidel.

The second project complemented the first. It would create in the Alejo Carpentier Cultural Center a discussion series on these new works, in which the painters, the critics, and an interested audience would participate. The idea was to bring about a learned and reflexive relationship between art and the public. I went to some of these sessions and met some members of the younger generation who were anxious to read much more than what our universities would teach them. For the most part, the people behind this opening now live abroad. The spaces that seemed to timidly open up were immediately shut down when politics erupted directly and systematically into the young people's discussions.

By 1987, I was the assistant editor, and later, the editor, of the journal Letras cubanas. This position put me in direct contact with writers of every generation and allowed me to further develop the literary criticism I had begun in the pages of *El caimán*. This sort of cultural work gradually became a professional activity; as a product of it I published works on narrative in various cultural journals in the country. The University of Havana offered me a job, but at that point I agreed to sign on only as an adjunct professor.

My great passion was still Dostoyevski's work, and I managed to turn my senior thesis into a book of essays, but *El novelista conspirador,* as the book is called, has still not emerged from publishing limbo, the final printing having been held up since 1991 for lack of paper, or so they say. A friend managed to send me a copy of the proofs, and I guard it dearly.

As I writer I was able to take part in the privilege of outings abroad, as they were officially known. I visited Mexico, then Romania. These trips were part of a system of benefits that writers could make use of, as could other special citizens whose social function had a special interest to the government. Being allocated one of these trips had to be interpreted as an award, because it allowed release from the asphyxiating intellectual, moral, and economic circle we lived in. Materially speaking, it was a chance to acquire a few of the basic necessities by saving up the scant "hard cash" pocket money they provided for food and transport.

Many of those who traveled received the privilege because of their proven experience with presenting a public image of the Revolution as paradise to foreign eyes; others of us, in fierce competition, received invitations or were sent because we had reached a degree of specialization in our fields and because we were sparing in our political comments. Being young had its advantages: It was believed to be advantageous to export an image of competent intellectuals formed under socialist education.

The results of these travels were not foreseen by Cuban institutions, however. Many of those who traveled abroad requested asylum or obtained long-term contracts so they could stay abroad as long as possible. This kind of exodus was a great loss for the country, especially in the fine arts.

A Journey Through Looking Glasses

On one of these trips, I arrived in Bucharest in the middle of 1990. The streets were still filled with strikers, and candles burned in the students' square in tribute to the jailed and murdered. Romania was an example of the consequences of having the pendulum swing too far in one direction, then letting it fall abruptly. No one trusted the inner resources of the country to keep away future dictators, nor to recover economically and morally. My guide would stop in front of each store window to show me the new Italian products on sale at incredibly high prices.

Corina—the guide—wanted to emigrate, as did the majority of young people with whom I spoke. It was distressing. Older people didn't encourage me, either. Old university professors and some of the writers and publication directors I had a chance to spend time with had taken refuge in domestic tranquility and the easing of shortages, or they dedicated themselves to planning vengeance on ancient rivals in power. I did not find the euphoria for reconstructing society that I had expected, but rather, enthusiasm for abandoning a boat that was sinking, full of wormholes, and too worn out to turn in new directions. I returned to Cojímar with a feeling of having taken a trip in a time machine. What I envisioned for Cuba, then and now, is more or less the same. You cannot expect that people worn out in a daily struggle for survival and trained in alienation from their rights as citizens by a dictatorship could turn, with a simple change of government, into a civil and democratic society over night.

Return to the Most Transparent City

When I had the chance to travel again, I went to Mexico City on a fellowship from the Colegio de México. When I got on the plane I had not decided to stay away from Cuba any longer than my studies required. A year and a half was the distance I needed to put between my battered country and the possibility of continuing to develop an independent way of thinking. I had begun to familiarize myself with the postmodernists and felt especially attracted to Michel Foucault, but my reading was disordered, chance borrowings, rushed. It was entering the Program in Interdisciplinary Women's Studies at the Colegio de México that allowed me to reorient myself theoretically and make a decision: I would not return to Cuba to beg for borrowed books.

For me, Mexico signified in many ways what we call "coming of age." The love-hate relation that tied me to Mexico during that first year was midwife to a completely different way of seeing the world, of positioning myself as a person in a place other than Home-and-Country. When I arrived I feared all the differences, the open spaces, the margins of the unforeseen. Cut off from the rituals of daily routine, I felt I had lost my center. Reading Agnes Heller, going from one metro stop to another, and learning to drink tequila with my new Mexican friends, I came to understand that only through a Dialog with my surroundings could I recover

Illustration 11.2. The author in Mexico City, 1992

my lost sense of the everyday. I turned everything into paths, then into goals, and finally into pleasures. Insignificant details acquired value once I began to feel the rhythm of the city and got used to its tensions and contrasts. Pity that at the height of the romance, as the bolero "Nosotros" would put it, Mexico and I had to part ways.

First, though, there was a lot that was good. With a work permit, the company of my daughter who had just arrived from Cuba, Frida (a cocker spaniel I had been given), and a minuscule apartment at the crest of the Olivar del Conde neighborhood, I felt happy, legal, and curious about that rich cultural world. I found time for my classes at the Colegio, for auditing Enrique Dussel's seminar in contemporary philosophy at the Universidad Nacional Autonoma de Mexico (UNAM), for collaborating at Editorial Era, at the newspaper *El Universal,* and at the journals *La Jornada Semanal, Plural,* and *Tierra Adentro.* These were Center-Left publications interested in the viewpoint of an intellectual who was formed by the Revolution but was critical of it.

Under these conditions of ideological pluralism, writing was a pleasure. In Mexico I was free because I felt responsible, and I decided that the objective of everything I wrote should be to create a public space for contemplating my country while keeping the right to return, to stay or to go. For me, that is the meaning of the word freedom for the Cuban intellectual abroad.

My articles were mainly on literary themes, but I became more and more directly interested in politics and began to work on two projects that remain unfinished. The first was Todo mezclado, "All Mixed Up," which would gather the writers from different generations, living on and off the island, who wanted to question the Option Zero that the Cuban government had officially put before the people.[3] Their responses would be published immediately in the cultural section of *El Universal;* but those from Havana never arrived. I showed three Cuban writers who were passing through Mexico City at the time the two sheets of paper on which I had formulated the project. They literally told me that I was "crossing the line," and they grew worried about me. I think they still are, sincerely.

The other project was "Letters to the Reader," for which I had gotten space in La Jornada. The idea was that those of us who were recent arrivals from Cuba would write chronicles in which we brought the Mexican public up to date on what was happening on the island from a perspective of debates. My friends, writers who were more or less established in Mexico, as well as students like myself, agreed to participate so long as they could use pseudonyms, but the editors of the newspaper's cultural section would not accept that condition. No one wanted to be compromised, and I understood perfectly, because I had also published before under the pseudonym of Eloísa Rodríguez Valdés in the pages of El Financiero. We were all afraid of losing the right to come and go from Cuba. The Cuban Embassy in Mexico, set up in an immense and luxurious building, kept an extensive yet refined control over the activities of Cubans living in the city. Any contempt of the established limits of censorship would be punished by cancellation of the permit for remaining abroad that the Cuban authorities had granted. That would leave four unpalatable possibilities: go back to Cuba in the knowledge that you would never again be allowed to travel; stay illegally in Mexico, which would immediately bring trouble from the Department of Immigration; head for the northern border and pay a coyote to get you across; or invent some whopper to tell the gringo embassy in the hope that they'd give you one of their prized visas.

Any one of these options meant losing that open space in Mexico—and not coincidentally. The Cuban government and cultural institutions are conscious of the importance of keeping a favorable public opinion in the most influential country in Latin America in terms of the continent's foreign policy toward Cuba. They were not about to allow a critical discourse that would provide an alternative to the official one in such a strategic terrain. This remains the challenge of an alliance with the Mexican intelligentsia:

to open spaces to circulate ideas about culture and politics that will start a new debate about Cuba.

Options Versus Crossroads

This is, among others, the kind of project that encouraged the "Third Option."[4] Some of us believe the Third Option is not located in any particular geographical space, nor tied to a single, predetermined political position. It can be defined as an attitude of resistance, a challenge to the magnetism of the dominant poles, a call for the individual's right to displacement, to doubt, to question ideologies. Those who worked for this line of thought in Cuba did so, generally speaking, through art. Rebelliousness sang, it painted, it wrote—all in complicity with metaphor and symbolism.

Many of these young writers, painters, and musicians gradually abandoned the country at the end of the 1980s when the opening in cultural institutions came to an end. At first this diaspora took place through student fellowships and invitations to mount exhibitions, give lectures, teach courses; whatever the means, it was a way to keep the door open for returning. This loophole, this door left conveniently ajar, began to close around 1989 to 1991. It soon closed altogether. I don't think it makes much difference now who bolted the latch. In some cases, pleading for asylum was a bureaucratic gesture, like marrying a foreigner or getting a residence permit to be able to work, but we began to stay abroad, and they, in Cuba, began to keep us out.

The worst part is that the different ways of staying abroad opened up a rift in our generation. The label of "exilio de terciopelo," "velvet exile," was given to those who retained permission to return to Cuba, even though they live in "third countries." In general their political statements were measured, and they never directly condemned the Cuban government. Those who imposed the label used it to mark their difference from the political ambiguity that characterized the "gusanos aterciopelados," "velveted worms," or "los quedaditos," "little stay-abroads," as the Cuban authorities call them.

This polarization has broken old friendships and damaged more than one project, because one group refuses to come together with the other. This is the generational dilemma for those of us who have grown creatively as intellectuals within a culture that is deterritorialized daily. We maintain strong sentimental ties to a nation more and more repressed by a totalitarian state. Why am I here, too, writing these pages under the last summer sun in Port Jefferson, Long Island, the place where I live with my daughter as a permanent resident of the State of New York?

Miami Does Not Believe in Tears[5]

Once in the United States, I decided not to ask for political asylum. I came to the United States when I became an illegal in Mexico. Cuban authorities in Mexico refused to renew my passport, a punishment for an article I published in Plural defending María Elena Cruz Varela, a Cuban poet and dissident. Through friends I managed to obtain a journalist visa to enter the United States.

I did not want to put myself in a situation that would rule out my legal return to Cuba, but, more importantly, I did not want to adulterate the content of my subversive actions, to usurp the right for protection that others had won fair and square. I had to face the astonishment and criticism of relatives and friends in Miami. I wasn't thinking clearly, they said.

As a result of my choice I could not get a work permit, and for nine months my daughter, my father, and I all lived from his meager salary as a hotel maintenance worker. The three of us shared an *efichienci,* as an efficiency apartment is called in the slang of the new arrivals. There was no money even to pay for air conditioning in the middle of summer. We slept by turns on a cot and a convertible sofa that I nicknamed "the Procrustean Bed." That August, I would paraphrase Eliot, was the cruelest month. No point in asking me if the gesture for which my loved ones suffered made sense, because whatever my answer might be now, at the time I couldn't have done anything else.

I confess that when I lived in Cuba, and even in Mexico, the possibility of ending up in Miami revolted me. I imagined it to be the nest of all the *gusanos*. I am grateful for the opportunity to change my mind, because it has enriched me humanely and politically. Miami has made me feel more Cuban, allowed me to reencounter a part of my country's past that I could not have found in the official history, to meet and respect people who before would have been dismissed as enemies, to integrate aspects of our national idiosyncrasy that have been banished by decree under socialism. It has taught me, as my friend, the writer Carlos Victoria, concluded, to be more tolerant precisely because I was facing people who could not be.

Nevertheless, after this apprenticeship I felt it was time to leave, for like any magic place, it should be set apart for ritual encounters alone. Miami would henceforth remain a place for meeting friends or family, for eating roast pork and downing grapes on New Year's Eve, or for escaping from northern snows to Miami Beach. It's the place to hear Albita's new CD or the latest joke from Havana, to enjoy a batido de mamey, sopa de plátano, or a yuca con mojo, to feel there's some spot to which we can still return, where something dear and homey waits to welcome us in when nostalgia plays us a dirty trick.

I only gained access to these sentimental benefits after an initiation period. During that time I felt worn down by the constant odor of political argument that keeps every Cuban busy from Kendall to the sagüesera. This odor is rancid at times and at times acrid, penetrating. It permeates the streets and the restaurants, it's transmitted over radio and television waves, it even reaches the press and theater. One man stars on every set: Fidel, or Castro as he is usually called in Miami. It starts to seem unreal, a mirage of the other Cuba, the other place where almost everyone curses the man, although quietly. At first I found this ridiculous, but time, which does not reduce the absurdity of it by one whit, does teach one to understand its causes.

The anonymous and pathetic stories that anyone you meet is ready to tell you at any time and place, of how they killed some woman's husband in the Bay of Pigs, or of the *balsero* or *balsera* who never reached shore, of the tortures and torments of political imprisonment, of the frustrations of those who arrive and cannot follow their own profession, of the pain of separated families: This molten lava of emotions feeds a hatred that I cannot share but can forgive. For them, thinking that "Castro is about to fall" is a kind of collective delirium, a firm desire that keeps people united in their identification as a community of exiles.

Precisely this phenomenon is one of the factors that make Miami a difficult enclave in which to work for political choices and cultural alternatives. It is not an apt space for accepting and cultivating difference or Dialog. Even so, I think that the city, for reasons of historical legitimacy, is an indispensable space for reconstructing the map of our fragmented nation. Not only because it has, for a whole century, gathered the majority of Cuban exiles, but also because in it a nearly perfect archive of Cuban culture has been forged, and it allows everyone access to its archaeology. Miami, apart from its expressways and McDonalds, has created and maintained the important language of memory, whose oppressive orality is at the same time a guarantee of its perpetual renovation.

The Island That Repeats Itself

I left Miami at the end of 1993 to finish my doctorate at Stony Brook, on Long Island, New York. A chain of old and new affections sustained me in the difficult but necessary transition to create a space in Long Island, which I call my other island, a cold place with harbors and seagulls.

Port Jefferson is the place I have lived stably for the longest time. After two years I surprised myself by calling it "my town." When friends visited me from other cities I had fun greeting them and seeing them off at the tiny train station. I learned where to buy the best Chinese food and even acquired some of the habits of the people who winter here. Nevertheless, a wall of words I never understood always separated me from what is called well-being. I managed to feel at home only rarely—at exceptional moments that depended on who was with me, what music I was listening to, or how the light streamed in through the window.

There is nothing unusual about what I am saying: This is the drama of thousands of immigrants in conflict with a foreign language. I always make fun of my ineffectual accent and clumsy ear, remembering how Heredia called English a "language of barbarous sounds"; but it is more than just a linguistic tic, this inability to pick up naturally on a newspaper article or a trivial conversation. Sometimes it has even been threatening, as when I had an operation in the Stony Brook University Hospital, and I found it so hard to struggle with both my fear of physical pain and my terror of not understanding the bill I'd have to pay or knowing how my insurance would cover it. Even today I don't understand a bit of it and stick to paying my five dollars a month so they won't bother me with their bills and letters: "You must know that your debt is in delinquency."

Nevertheless, I have made great progress. I managed something as significant as learning to drive a car, so dangerous for someone who feels she is floating in reality. Driving has been a healthy exercise in adapting to my environment. I became just another person driving my old Dodge convertible around the main street of Port Jefferson. I was also just another person when I went to the meetings at Lena's school and confirmed that I have nothing to fear for my daughter.

Lena has grown to adolescence in another language, another culture, but she has continued to be a sweet, sagacious child with whom I can talk about so many things. At times we joke about whether she has become a *gringa,* and with laughter I exorcize a danger that she does not feel. National identity is not a problem when you are thirteen. It is a natural, flowing process, a mixture of roots and fresh blooms. I've always tried to stay close to her and to have the privilege of being the first to discover her changes, understand them, follow their course as far as possible. I hope that this habit will not come to an end and that our password for communication can be updated if necessary.

Five years will soon have passed since I came to the United States, and I'm not sure when I will be able to go back to Cuba. Letters, faxes, go-betweens carrying my requests for academic visas to the Cuban institutions that could grant them have all gone unanswered. Where have all those words come to rest? Is there any Dialog left to attempt? I don't know.

In the meantime I've decided that, if I go back, it will be with a tourist visa to visit Cuba.[6] I will join the anonymous line of old exiles (and a few recent arrivals) who pretend they are going to Cancún or Nassau for a tan in order to land at last at the airport in Rancho Boyeros. I think I'll buy myself a white diaphanous linen dress and a little straw hat for the debut of this persona. No matter; when I get to Havana I hope they'll recognize me, because, among other things, that is why I'm going, so they'll say to me, "Chica, you haven't changed a bit." I'm going to confirm my identity, psychologists and sociologists would say.

Who knows? At least I think I want to measure with my own senses what's been happening there while I've been gone, let myself be marked by the uncertainty and hope with which Cubans live, and feel that what happens there makes a difference to me and involves me. I read in a little santería handbook that it is worth it to trade everything you know for everything you haven't yet learned. I want to learn how to visit Cuba, because I already know what it is to live in Cuba and what it is to live without Cuba. In the meantime, I can critique Albert Hirschman. According to his thesis, dissident intellectuals in the contemporary world have only two options: exit or voice.[7] Here, too, I want to bet on a third option, because leaving doesn't have to mean staying away, and in order to give voice, you might need other spaces, other interlocutors.

Notes

1. Mercedes Sosa en Argentina, Polygram Records, 1994.
2. "Happiness Is the Barrel of a Warm Gun," White Album, 1979.

3. Option Zero, the government's cut-back plan. It's a worst-case scenario.

4. On the origin and development of these groups and activities, see the Master's thesis of Lilian Martínez, *Intelectuales y poder político en Cuba: La "intelectualidad de la ruptura" y el "proceso de rectificación"* (FLASCO, Mexico City, June 1992). See also, among other texts, the anthology, *Cuba: La isla posible,* edited by Juan Pablo Ballester, María Elena Escalona, and Ivánde la Nuez (Barcelona: Centre de Cultura Contemporánia and Ediciones Destino, 1995); the journal *Plural* (no. 250, 1992); and my essay, "Third Option: Beyond the Borders" (*Michigan Quarterly Review*, 33[4]: 217–224, Fall 1994).

5. This heading alludes to the Soviet film, *Moscow Does Not Believe in Tears*, a prominent piece of Soviet communist cinema.

6. Tourist visa to visit Cuba for those born there.

7. Hirschman, Albert. *Exit, Voice, and Loyalty: Responses to Decline in Firms, Organizations, and States*. Cambridge, Mass.: Harvard University Press, 1970.

12

Postwar Memories
Tania Bruguera

Ana Mendieta

AN ARTIST is a space for communication. In the artist, reality comes together, and through the artist, ideas are received and transmitted. These ideas are part of a moment that returns, and then other artists retake those ideas and carry them forward.

The artwork of Ana Mendieta was part of a conference that I attended in 1986. Ana Mendieta was born in Cuba but left at the age of twelve for the United States. I had seen images of her artwork, and they had impressed and fascinated me, but it was at this conference that I learned she had died. A feeling of loss seized me. It seemed unjust that such a powerful body of art should be left incomplete.

I wanted to make an homage. I began to look for her. Her death had frustrated any attempt to meet her. I searched for her through her artwork, through the marks she had left on those who knew her. I imagined that I could eliminate the idea of her death if her artwork could continue. I tried to understand and to learn.

Beyond her artwork, Ana then became a symbol of returning to the homeland. Being a symbol meant also the possibility of somehow belonging, the possibility of having at least the right to belong. Within Cuba, her return became the proof that there really was another part of us that existed, even if we didn't know it.

Illustration 12.1. Homage to Ana Mendieta

This happened almost as a premonition of what would come next, when many of those who had known her changed their status with regard to Cuba, when it was our turn to lose friends, relatives, and partners in the later "disappearances." Ana had tried to ignore her "non-existent" condition. She and her exile became the metaphor for the defining conflict of my generation: Can you belong without being there? The questions I asked myself in order to understand Ana, I could later ask about each new person who left.

I realized that the most important thing was to rescue Ana from oblivion, not only because of what she represented, but also because of the way she understood how to make Cuban art, to recover its essence. The artwork I wanted to make through Ana's

artwork was more a cultural gesture than a manufacturing of objects. The object was the point of reference. I was just the ar-
chaeologist, the medium. The action was to incorporate her, to
make her part of the cultural context, of the reference. It was to
give her a time and a place within Cuba, within Cuban art. And
what better way to do that than through her artwork? What better homage than to recognize that this was also a way of representing us? What better way to continue the Dialog?

Memory of the Postwar Period

In 1993 the average address book came to have only a few names
and phone numbers that could still be read among all the crossed-
out lines. Starting over, getting to know new people, getting involved again: How long could this go on?

Trying not to erase old memories, which by then were more
idealized, of course, I discovered that the legacy of the artists who
had left now belonged almost exclusively to the realm of memory
and oral history. There were very few tangible signs of what they
had done.

Since this was the medium—which no longer existed for those
people who had left—in which I trained as an artist, I wished to
comment on my new landscape in the manner that those artists
who had left had done with theirs when they lived in Cuba. I
wished to recover a certain time, a certain atmosphere, and to test
whether it was still possible to use certain themes that they had
used in their artworks. I reedited their icons, their strategies: the
flags, the performances, the discussions, the interchange, the island, the politics, the defiance, the social commentary.

I remember that in art history classes at school the social
panorama of past eras was taught through artists' works. Teachers tried to explain those artworks as a reaction in some sense to
what was happening around the artists, a point of reference, a
commentary on their lives. In the Cuban history classes, repeated
year after year with little variation, they spoke to us—some with

more, some with less passion—about the privilege of living and participating in a historical moment. They made us conscious of the benefits we enjoyed thanks to the heroism of others.

I thought I could assume the post of artist as witness who would leave a record of the social upheavals of the era. I wanted to try to put to the test the theory of art as agent of change of reality.

The name of this series of works is Memory of the Postwar Period. I used postwar as a metaphor of the circumstances within Cuban art after the wave of emigration of artists in the late 1980s and early 1990s, an emigration that left among the artists in Cuba a confused sensation of being mistaken; I used postwar as metaphor for the results of a "war" between art and power that had, for the moment, finished its most frontal phase; and I used postwar as a metaphor for the similarity at the physical level of the city, for people's inner lives, for the new social role of art.

Memory, not to forget continuity.

The artworks that make up this series became a personal, intimate collective experience, because although each of us has had to personally resolve the conflicts it depicts at a personal level at some time, they also represent conflicts we experienced in common.

Memory of the Postwar Period is also the name of one artwork that synthesizes the idea of this series. It is the point that holds together the need to think of culture as a collective occurrence and of art as a gesture. It appears as a newspaper, because one can see in it a testimonial space that presents notes rather than theses in its commentaries; because it is a point of reference for opinions; because of its assembled character; and because of the immediacy of its need for self-expression. Even though by the time we read it, a newspaper's way of framing things, of responding to them, of explaining them may not be the same, it continues to have historical value that resides in the possibility it gives us to know what was being thought at a given time and place and to find out what had happened from the voice of a witness.

The strategy of this artwork lies in its mimetic force, its existence on the borders of its own illusions, its virtual coherence in its way of appearing and circulating, the confusion, the gesturality, its role, the desire not to lose the testimony while a moment was being crystallized.

This artwork was assembled on two occasions, each time with a central theme. The first was the postwar period as symbolic condition of the situation within art; the second, on emigration. I tried to begin a discussion and leave a record about matters that I felt were at that moment blurred in public opinion at the same time that they were themes or places of coincidence in the investigations of various artists or theorists. The collaborators were artists, critics, curators, researchers, gallery owners, art students—

Illustration 12.2. Studio work for series Memory of the Postwar Period

generally, everyone who took part in the world of the production or circulation of art.

This artwork owes a debt to its place of origin, Cuba, and to the moment that it lived within Cuban culture. One of its main objectives was not to exclude anyone from either side of the sea, but rather to be a bridge, a neutral space for coming together.

The Trip

The Trip is an artwork that is like a ritual. Every element that formed part of my past and every object that contained the memories of times past were broken and packed into brown paper bags, and the bags tied with ropes of twine by which they could be held if one wanted to carry them, as one carries what one lives.

Within the bags were maps that helped me find certain ethical roads that I followed, or that turned out to be false: books that led me to other places; drawings that had accumulated; clothes; debris from my house in construction, trash from the very exhibition in which the artwork was being shown.

Illustration 12.3. The Trip

One of the most important elements was the correspondence I had kept up for almost twenty months with the man who had been, up to then, my companion of six years. He had decided to take a trip to Mexico, and the trip back kept being delayed as he asked for new exit permits and new visas and then repeating the permit requests, until the meaning of his presence in that place began to change. We gradually came to understand that he had emigrated, one more who had decided that this was the chosen way to resolve certain conflicts, part of a feverish joint aspiration in which, possibly, all of us took part.

The first exhibition at which I showed this artwork tried to analyze the different ways of resolving both the social situation and the artistic position through various personal moments. This artwork was placed at the end of the line, next to the door, ready to be taken as hand luggage or to be seen as an accumulation of memories that has been taken out or that is already in that strange dimension of belonging outside of ourselves. It is an artwork that tries to capture an instant, to freeze an action.

Later, I began to see the relation between what had happened to me and many other people's stories: friends who had used letters as a means of communication and people who had left in one way or another forever and who needed to perform a similar ritual, although under other, more insurmountable pressures, such as having to leave the country where they were born and having to pay for it with acts of renunciation of what they had been.

That was when I decided that the next time it was exhibited, I would change its condition of accumulation for that of the island of Cuba. It would be a metaphor for the island built through the act of renunciation, the renunciation by others of its past, of its future. It was a metaphor for the price of an island made from the memories of so many lives lived and packed away for the time when they could come back to pick them up. My memories were transformed into a simile for the memories of those who had left the country. The gesture I had made, my personal experience, had gained a new dimension. Just as they had taught us in school, our past life came to form part of a process, a collective development; each one of us contained the concept; each one of us was the country.

Life Raft

The Life Raft is a project (as it can only aspire to a work of art), a monument to those who have died trying to get to the other side. It is a funerary artwork: Black marble is used for the lifesaving planks; their size represents the average height of a person in Cuba, 1.65 meters [or 5 feet 5 inches]. Between each slab of marble, a timber forms a line that suggests half the structure of a boat. The image can only be completed when this skeleton is united with its reflection in the marble. Between each plank is cotton for caulking so the boat will not sink; it is a healing element, a sign of salvation. All this is in a repeating structure, suggesting an unpredictable finitude, anonymous, incapable of naming any of those who form this space, becoming a monument to silence.

Illustration 12.4. Life Raft

Fear

Fear was an obsessive act in which I first drew near the island (The Trip) and picked up one of the bags. I took out the cotton and held it while walking toward the monument (Life Raft). I began using the cotton over and over to caulk the planks of that "boat," with the hope of thus "avoiding" capsizing. The cotton was a symbol of the desire to absolve all the pain so that it would disappear, so as to avoid it. After determining my frustrated intention, I went toward a boat, broken and laden with the history of its own uselessness, docked in a shipyard. I put into it the rest of the cotton from the bag, a bottle, and my body.

It was a trip without point of departure or point of arrival, which was death, just as it was a dream. My action was an offering, just as it was a desperate solution.

Statistic

Statistic is a funerary flag. The idea originally took shape as a wall on which I would place, like the marks that prisoners make in their cells, hair from anonymous Cubans, grouped into small locks and tied with thread. Later, trying to make a direct reference to Cuba, I drew on one of the motifs used by Cuban artists, particularly those of the 1980s generation: the flag.

The base is black fabric. On one side, the hair, tied together with red, white, and olive-green threads, substitutes for the real colors of the flag. On the other side, the black thread with which the hair is sewn to the fabric shows, black on black, the flag's pattern. It becomes one of those banners that are placed outside a house to indicate mourning.

I used hair because it is an element that in Cuban culture, as in almost every culture, is considered the place where all the energy, all the force of thought of a person concentrates. This is why, in the Afro-Cuban religion, the hair is one of the parts of the living body that is most often used for controlling someone's "head,"

Illustration 12.5. Statistic

their thoughts, their decisions. In this case, tying them down is done literally, with the threads.

This is an artwork with the force of ritual, which moves from the action of looking for the hair and rolling it up to sitting down every day for months to sew the Cuban flag, as in the colonial era. In that era the women of the household would gather or they would go to another patriot's house, and they would sit down to sew this same flag, which at the time was not the national emblem but a standard of revolutionary and independent ideas. It was an act of conspiracy and solidarity. It helped them to feel useful while the men were at war.

During the nearly four months that we were making this work, each time some friend came to visit the house, my assistant, Peria, and I would give them a needle and we would explain to them the idea behind the work and what had to be done. We talked about everything.

This flag has another part, which is made from the perspective of those Cubans who live outside Cuba.

Head Down

Head Down takes its name from a poem and the title of a book by the Cuban poet, Carlos A. Alfonso. It was first exhibited at the alternative gallery, Espacio Aglutinador, in Havana.

A trench separates the public from the space where the performance unfolds. The floor is carpeted with artists, critics, art and art history students, people of the world of art. As in other artworks, the audience at whom the work is directed is part of it, the subject of study, of analysis, of discussion.

Everyone is sprawled on the floor, face down, on his or her sides, every which way, on top of each other. The only person not in this position stands waiting patiently next to some flags. Personal and sexual traits scarcely exist, eliminated by a coating of flour. From the back, emerging from the imitation lamb's wool vestment and raising up over the person's head, is a banner, a banner just like the ones that lay about on the floor. It is incorporated, like those banners of the Japanese samurai, who put on flags according to the new lords for whom they have to fight and conquer and defend territories.

The background music begins. It is played by the experimental sound group from ICAIC, the Cuban Cinematic Arts and Industry Institute, and the songs are of the Cuban Nueva Trova movement, symbols of the new revolutionary ethics.

The principal character takes a flag and begins to walk over the bodies sprawled on the floor. She stops, stoops to get closer to the bodies, to one in particular; she ties on a ribbon of the same color as the flags, takes a banner just like the one she carries on her back,

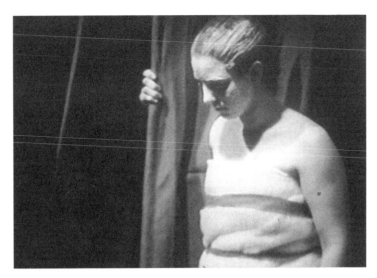

Illustration 12.6. Head Down

and keeps walking on top of these people. She stops, stoops to reach one of the bodies, and ties on a ribbon that is clearly a piece of the flag, using it to cover the mouth. She rises, drives in the symbol of her triumph—a flag, which the body stretched on the ground has to hold up. She marks her own body by tying a ribbon onto it, too, as a trophy after the victorious action. These actions are repeated: tying up the eyes, the hands, the ears, the mouths, the feet of the others, always leaving her triumphal banner and marking her body with a ribbon.

The "conquered territories" then begin to modify the landscape. There are two views, one in which the spectator can see from above all that has been described and another in which the public sees only a phantasmagoric character, who walks around creating a setting of red flags until at last she breaks through the encirclement formed by the trench. With flags and ribbons in hand, the character advances, beginning to perform the same action on those bodies who are watching the performance, on the public itself. She disappears.

The people who were strewn about the floor slowly begin to rise, throw off the flags and ribbons, and abandon the set.

Daedalus, or Empire of Salvation

When I left Cuba for the first time, I was an adult, and I went to England on a two-month fellowship. They gave me a study and a space for exhibiting the results of what I created there. Like any other artist under these conditions, I was drawn to the museums. I soon found myself looking at works of art that I had never dreamed of seeing in the original. In my delirium I remembered my friends, my students, my family—with all of them I had used many of the pieces I was now looking at as references, as objects of study, as comparisons, as commentaries, as points of departure.

Specifically, I recalled a student who at that time was creating art full of references to Brueghel the elder, and there I was, standing in front of the piece on which he was basing his work. I felt a kind of impotence, thinking that the student was the one who should be there, getting so much more benefit out of it for his own work, growing before these other pieces. I began to wish that he was there, and then I wished that another of my students could be there. I recalled many people I wished could be there with me, who could have had that opportunity.

Then I created flying devices—for leaving Cuba. I began to enumerate the possible ways of getting out. Each one became a device, each one an attempt.

Icarus had been a reference in an earlier work. Thinking of all the nuances of this mythical symbol, I remembered that in an exhibition in the National Museum of Fine Arts in Havana, an artist had based a piece on this figure in the 1980s, before the artists of his generation had decided to emigrate definitively. Icarus fell onto a surface of broken mirrors (broken at the moment of impact?) in this artist's installation. I remembered how appropriate the symbol was for representing what was happening back then, but those mirrors no longer reflected the way we—the artists living in Cuba and those who later emerged—now assume the act of leaving Cuba.

Searching for the roots of the myth, Icarus appeared next to the inventor of the wings, Daedalus. They were father and son. Both were trapped on an island, prisoners of their own movements, of their former loyalties, inside the labyrinth that Daedalus himself had constructed for the same King who now condemned them to be devoured by the Minotaur like any other enemy. With help, they managed to escape their own prison. They reached the shores of the island, but there was no other way out but the infinite, impossible sea. Daedalus, the inventor, used all his talents, all his knowledge, all his tricks to flee. He built wings for the two of them, warning his son about approaching too closely to the sun. The warning was a metaphor for the attitude with which one should assume this action. Icarus died because of his youthful and inexperienced anxiety. Daedalus, with more experience, watched painfully as his son fell and was lost. His attitude allowed him to continue, with this image of warning, to the shores of other kingdoms.

The image of Icarus was transformed in line with the way many had had to burn their own ships to be able to leave Cuba. Daedalus, who learned the lesson, who kept his distance, who recognized his advantages and his limitations, created his own means of escape. Just like him we have learned how to assume the risk of leaving Cuba by another means.

Each of the pieces that make up this series shows a way of constructing the possibility of leaving Cuba. This is only discovered when the device, which has been hung on the wall, camouflaged like one more part of the landscape, reveals its purpose when someone decides to put it on, when someone "activates" it by putting it on. The way the device has to be held, how the body has to mimic its motions, is how one discovers how to escape from the labyrinth and how to choose the actions that can make it possible for us to adopt a position of departure.

The devices are made from discarded material, found objects. In Cuba nothing is thrown away, everything becomes prime material for fixing something else that is broken. I wanted to adopt the attitude of the National Movement of Inventors. They are in charge of fixing up old and almost unusable machinery with whatever is at hand by substituting mechanisms and pieces from other machines. I thought of my character as part of this association. These devices would be the prototypes for mass production and would be distributed to all Cubans to be used for leaving Cuba.

A few examples:

- Absolution is made with leaves of the royal palm, the symbol of Cuba. It opens up with the person who carries it, folds, bends, worships.
- Illusion is a transformed bicycle, covered in parts with paper. When it is carried, the body takes the position of closed fists

Illustration 12.7. Daedalus, or Empire of Salvation #1

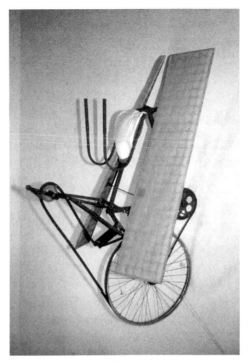

Illustration 12.8. Daedalus, or Empire of Salvation #2

held high. The weight of the steel is the symbolic equivalent of the burden of undertaking such a decision.

Another device is a corset of metallic cloth in which we put the body. It only begins to move when another person, who has put on the gloves connected to the figure, moves his or her fingers and begins to move the strings of power.

These are artworks in which a certain fragility coexists with weightiness to speak of the condition of leaving Cuba.

Art in America (The Dream)

In 1997, I was selected along with four other artists, for a two-month resident fellowship in the United States. Each of us went

Illustration 12.9. Daedalus, or Empire of Salvation #3

to a different city. Mine was Chicago. The myths among artists about being in the United States, of exhibiting there—and this is not exclusive to Cubans—is a whole history of well-founded ideas, of prejudices, of predispositions, and of false beliefs, all of which made me think of the title of this piece.

When I arrived at the School of the Art Institute, among other things they recited to me was a list of people that I would supposedly know, because they are connected to art. Among the names I recognized was Nereida García-Ferraz, a person I had tried to meet, because I remembered her as one of the makers of a documentary film about Ana Mendieta that had greatly impressed me and had been one of the reasons propelling me to make the piece on Ana.

I called her that very afternoon and went to see her. Kaky Mendieta was there, Ana's cousin, who had given me vital facts about Ana for my work. We spent the whole time talking about Cuba while we ate, about the Cuba she had left three years earlier, about the Cuba I had just come from, about the Cuba where we once lived, in our memories; they were all the same, all different.

They began introducing me to the people who formed part of their community, which, like all communities, is particular to its own circumstances. It was rather like a kind of circle, like a trip that begins and ends at the same point. I was with people who were family and friends of Ana Mendieta, friends who shared parts of her everyday life, her achievements, her final moments.

This was the first time I had lived inside a Cuban community in the United States. I saw how it really functioned, how it did and did not fit the myths that exist about such communities. For the first time my work on emigration changed its reference point; now it was not about the loss in Cuba, it was about the loss of Cuba.

This coincided with a tour I made of the city with some friends so that I might appreciate some of the local architecture as well as some of the more interesting, if lesser known, sights. At one point they explained that the city was multilayered, with different levels along the lake shore and beyond that served a multitude of purposes, both planned and unplanned.

On one of those levels, there is a road that goes underground and winds around the very foundations of the city. Along that road there is a submerged city, a place where human beings take refuge from the cold. The people who live there along the margins and without walls are homeless.

I became fascinated with this notion of a city within a city: on the top, visible; on the bottom, free of the problems of weather but invisible to the traffic whizzing by, a landscape of bedding in which the chairs, rather than places of rest, serve as watch posts next to cardboard boxes that give the illusion of living rooms, bedrooms—in short, a home.

I was especially impressed by the similarities between homeless and immigrant groups in the way, in order to protect themselves, they create trenches around the communities they build, devising their own "safe" spaces in which they maintain their own language, traditions, culture, and ways of being from past lives. These communities also function as a city within the city, as a city under the city.

In Cuba, as in most countries, the housing situation is one of the most oppressive problems, although for the moment at least there are no homeless people, either as individuals or as a social group. So Lower Wacker seemed a different world to me, but as I began to spend time there, the name given to the people of Lower Wacker—homeless—echoed for me the literal translation of the Spanish word *patria,* homeland. The relationship between these concepts of home and land to define a concept rendered more abstractly in other languages created a connection for me between the homeless and the homeland. Immigrants, like the homeless on Lower Wacker, lack a home on their own land.

As I began to think about the two groups, I realized there were other connections between their situations. Both communities have to convert their nomadic existences into a way of life. Both suffer from a certain loss of citizenship: the homeless, because they exist in a kind of no-man's-land, and the immigrants—to my thinking, Cuban immigrants in particular—because by leaving they abdicated their right to return and thus became a kind of pariah.

The harsh conditions of survival experienced by those who leave their homeland are often comparable to those experienced by people who lose their jobs, are thrown out of their homes, or suffer discrimination by the larger society. Both groups suffer from internal strife, sudden change, the need to assimilate quickly to new conditions, and the nearly fatal knowledge that it is practically impossible to change their situation. Both groups must also contend with an overwhelming bureaucracy that is often indifferent if not also inefficient.

The loneliness of both immigrants and the homeless when they arrive in a new place and have to re-establish themselves is also quite similar. Both must develop new skills, if for no other reason than they are both out of their natural habitats. Their destinies are no longer of their own making, their rights are few and mostly unknown to them. Immigrants, even when they accomplish the immediate goals of their journey, maintain, like the homeless, a certain sense of not belonging, of Other-ness.

Nostalgia is another point of commonality. The homeless yearn for a time when they had a home, a job, a family; the immigrant longs for a time, held in memory, that was always better. The impossibility of returning to the past serves as a kind of stigma for both groups. The struggle to return to the former way of life, both abstractly and concretely, begins to form their new way of life. Of course, not all Cubans emigrate for the same reasons, just as not all homeless people arrive at their condition for the same reasons. But both groups suffer oppressive social discrimination and at best are the objects of pity from those above.

Up to this point, my work had dealt with immigration from the perspective of someone living in Cuba and contending with its immediate effects on life there. I have now tried to approach the subject form a different perspective, taking into account the immigrant's own context and losses. There was much more to be explored and learned here, but this was at least a beginning.

In a performance I did, the participants included Ricardo Fernández, Nereida García-Ferraz, Raquel Mendieta, Achy Obejas, Alejandra Piers-Torres, Paola Piers-Torres, and Nena Torres. The majority of them are Cuban immigrants who left the island under different circumstances at different times. The piece was performed on a dark set with only a few yellow lights, in an effort to simulate the tunnel where the homeless live. There were several characters. To enter you had to pass a table where a person with a strict and official air asked you to leave a piece of identification in order to pass, as is done for legal transactions. It was explained that this was a necessary condition for proceeding. It was important that this function as a symbolic dispossession of the persons we all are or think we are, because of what we do socially, such as not letting certain things be seen.

Another character was set to moving cardboard boxes, named for parts of a house, which kept changing places and kept being made to serve in lieu of a real house. Every time he finished making his new dwelling he had once more to move it all to another place, endlessly. This action, beyond representing the instability of the immigrant's condition, was a metaphor for the constant search for the lost home.

In another corner a small girl stood with two women who read cards by the light of a candle, which as offering and as illumination let them see the future of passersby. The girl begged for food with a poster. The women were trying to collect money with the only thing they had managed to bring with them to this place where they now stayed, their only fortune, their spirituality, their traditions. The cards were read in Spanish by one woman and translated by the other into English; this was a metaphor for the effort that has to be made to understand other cultures, and to try to preserve one's own, which is our only shield.

To leave at the end, when your identification was returned, you had to pass through a process similar to that of the emigrants when they apply for citizenship in their country of residence. The same questions were asked as in the examination for U.S. citizenship. In many cases the audience, who were mainly U.S. citizens, gave the same answers and the same reactions that a real immigrant would give in the real process. People felt the same need to recover their own identity, the same compulsion to finish and leave without having to worry any more about this torturous situation. This is a work in progress.

I have returned to the United States for four months, and although there is a tremendous difference between what I am going through and the real life of an immigrant, I am having some similar experiences that help me understand personally some of the emotional and practical events that those who have to adapt after emigrating must go through.

Just as Ana wanted to return, conscientiously, to discover a part of her history that was not entirely accessible to her, and took her body as the measure of the world, so have I turned this stay abroad, this process, into a way of entering the life dynamics of a Cuban leaving Cuba; and I have taken my situation as a reference point, searching from the personal for a more complete vision and being more ready to understand Cubans as we are, in two parts.

About the Contributors

Eduardo Aparicio is a photographer, writer, and translator currently living in Chicago.

Liz Balmaseda is a columnist for the *Miami Herald*, Pulitzer Prize winner, and co-author, with Joe Greer, of *Waking Up In America*. She lives in Miami.

Tania Bruguera is a visual and performance artist who was awarded a Guggenheim Fellowship in 1998. Her work has been exhibited widely at the Venice, Italy; Johannesburg, South Africa; Sao Paolo, Brazil; and Havana Biennials. She was included in Documenta 2002. She is currently a professor of Performance and Visual Arts at Cuba's Art Institute. She lives in Havana.

Madelín Cámara is a professor of Hispanic Literature at Southern Florida University and co-editor of *Cuba, the Elusive Nation: Interpretations of National Identity*.

Carmen Díaz is a former physics professor at the University of Havana and is currently a clinical psychologist in Miami.

Josefina de Diego is the author of the poem *"En el reino de mi abuelo"* and numerous other short stories and poems. She lives in Havana.

Teresa de Jesús Fernández is a professor of Hispanic Literature at the University of Sassari in Italy and author of *La Poesia de revolucion*.

David Frye is an anthropologist, writer, and translator who lives in Ann Arbor, Michigan.

Nereida García-Ferraz has received numerous awards for her photography and paintings. She was coproducer of the video "Ana Mendieta: Fuego de tierra." She is currently living in Florida.

Ana Mendieta, visual and performing artist, died in September 1985.

Raquel Mendieta Costa was formerly a professor of Cuban cultural history at the Cuban Art Institute and is the author of *Cultura: Lucha de clases y conflicto racial 1878–1895* and numerous articles on Cuban culture. She was also a member of the editorial board of *Propociones,* a short-lived but influential cultural magazine published in Cuba in the early 1990s.

Achy Obejas is the cultural citric of the *Chicago Tribune* and author of *Mambo Memory, We Came All the Way from Cuba so You Can Dress Like That?* and *Days of Awe.*

Mirta Ojito, former staff writer for the *New York Times,* is working on a book about the Mariel boat lift. She lives in Miami.

María de los Angeles Torres is an associate professor of political science at De Paul University, author of *In the Land of Mirrors: Cuban Exiles Politics in the U.S.*, and co-editor of *Borderless Borders: Latinos, Latin Americans, and the Paradoxes of Interdependence.*